CATALYTIC FORMATIONS

First published 2006
by Taylor & Francis

Published 2016 by Routledge
2 Park Square, Milton Park, Abingdon, Oxon OX14 4RN
711 Third Avenue, New York, NY 10017

Routledge is an imprint of the Taylor & Francis Group, an informa business

Cover Image: Contemporary Architecture Practice
Cover Design: Dean Di Simone
Graphic Design Director: Dean Di Simone
Graphic Production: Florence Production

Typeset in Helvetica Neue by
Florence Production Ltd, Stoodleigh, Devon

The publisher makes no representation, express or implied, with regard to the accuracy of the information contained in this book and cannot accept any legal responsibility or liability for any errors or omissions that may be made.

British Library Cataloguing in Publication Data
A catalogue record for this book is available from the British Library

Library of Congress Cataloging in Publication Data
A catalog record for this book has been applied for

ISBN 13: 978-1-138-22810-8 (pbk)

CATALYTIC FORMATIONS ARCHITECTURE AND DIGITAL DESIGN

ALI RAHIM

Routledge
Taylor & Francis Group

LONDON AND NEW YORK

Facade Detail. Inflecting Potential: Commercial Office Tower, Dubai, UAE

CONTENTS

Study Model. Migrating Coastlines: Residential Housing Tower, Dubai, UAE

DESIGN PROJECTS

00 INTRODUCTION

In the last twenty years, the digital revolution has accelerated cultural change at a rate and to an extent unparalleled since the Industrial Revolution. Digital technologies have the potential to profoundly transform architecture practices and techniques. Since the early 1990s, pioneering architects such as Frank Gehry and Greg Lynn have been exploring the implications of computing technologies on the design and production of architecture.[01] The most radical experiments in design and computing, however, have remained largely sequestered in academic institutions and a few boutique offices. Today, the vast majority of architects limit their engagements with electronic media to the use of a limited palette of computer-based production tools. Software such as FormZ, 3D Studio MAX, and AutoCAD are employed by many conventional architecture practices as tools for representing a design after it has been developed or conceived. Computer applications such as CATIA and Rhinoceros allow architects to perform curvature analysis or to determine potential bending stress and material strain calculations more rapidly than in the past. The incorporation of computer-based technologies as tools of representation and analysis has led to important advances for the discipline. Yet architecture can and must go further. In this book, I investigate another approach, one that sees digital technologies as platforms from which architects can develop new techniques, giving rise to innovative works of architecture with significant cultural effects.

Innovation is not merely change but change that sustains lasting cultural effects. Innovation is a development that people find useful or meaningful. To be innovative, architects—and works of architecture themselves—must become more responsive to their users and environments. In other words, they must incorporate feedback from their physical and cultural contexts rather than relying solely on conventional analytical or internal processes of development. The idea of feedback applies to every aspect of architectural production, from design to construction. Feedback provides a means to evaluate architecture's effects and to promote further transformation—and thus is a theme that recurs throughout this book.

How do architects generate feedback? This is where recent digital technologies can play an important role. By using new software and fabrication technologies that build in mechanisms for generating feedback, architects can develop techniques to create more dynamic forms of architecture—dynamic not in the sense that they literally move but because they are activated through interactions with their users and contexts. Since they continually rely on feedback from participants, such works are open-ended and always contain the potential to give rise to new, unexpected effects. These effects may include the evolution of new techniques and technologies, drawing architecture into a larger feedback loop of technological and cultural development.

Catalytic Formations: Architecture and Digital Design describes how architects can more effectively engage recent technological developments to produce forms of architecture that generate feedback from their users and within culture at large. In short, this book identifies methods to promote innovation in the practice and design of architecture. Readers, however, should not look for a predetermined series of steps that will enable them to participate in the current digital milieu. This is not a manual or handbook.

Neither does it conform to the established types of architectural publications; instead it interlaces theories, images, and descriptions of projects that share a common set of themes. Unlike many architecture books, this publication focuses as much on the process of design as on the outcome, arguing that how a work develops is integral to its effects in the world.

The book is organized as a set of three trajectories that move at different speeds, allowing readers a degree of flexibility in approaching it. The first trajectory spans the entire arc of the book and traces the feedback loop linking architecture, technology, and culture. I begin by laying the groundwork for understanding the relationship between technology and architectural techniques. Techniques that incorporate technology to effectively generate feedback are necessary for the development of innovative design practices. Two aspects of these techniques are examined in particular: temporality and virtuality. I show how designers use techniques that incorporate temporality and virtuality to create works of architecture capable of generating feedback with their users and environments, leading potentially to larger cultural effects. These dynamic works of architecture are what I call *catalytic formations*. Finally, this large feedback loop between technologies, techniques, architecture, users, contexts, and culture is projected into the future. Feedback becomes a means to evaluate emerging technologies that may shape architectural practice in the years to come. Throughout the book, the process of working with feedback is contrasted with conventional design methods, which tend to be more linear and predictable. I call this first trajectory slow because it encompasses the book as a whole, and understanding all of the relationships and connections within this large feedback loop may require reading the volume once—or even multiple times.

A second series of medium-speed trajectories is found within the book's chapters. Each chapter traces the feedback between two specific concepts, which are illustrated and developed through examples from past and current design practices—ranging from projects by the mid-century American designers Charles and Ray Eames to designs by contemporary practitioners such as Zaha Hadid Architects, Greg Lynn FORM, Cecil Balmond of Arup, dECOi, KOL/MAC Studio, and NOX. These projects all generate interactive responses with their users and environments, and thus illustrate the larger feedback loop between techniques, formations, and catalytic effects. Chapter 01, *Techniques and Technology*, unravels how design practices invent new techniques to take advantage of technological developments. I designate as *technological* those design practices that effectively use techniques to produce innovative designs, and offer two historical examples: the designers Charles and Ray Eames and Verner Panton, all important innovators of their respective periods. Through these examples, I enumerate the features common to technological practices, including the requirement that they use techniques generated in their contemporary contexts. For architects today, this means embracing and exploring the potential offered by digital techniques.

Chapter 02, *Temporality and Time*, elaborates on the digital techniques available today, focusing in particular on their relationship to time and temporality. I define as *temporal techniques* methodologies that implicitly subscribe to an open-ended and "irreversible" model of time borrowed from thermodynamics. Two kinds of temporal techniques are highlighted in particular: generative and transformational methods that draw on software borrowed from the automotive and film industries. The use of a thermodynamic model of temporality leads architecture practices to think of themselves as agile, flexible organizations that transform over time.

In Chapter 03, *Virtual and Actual*, I explore the concept of the *virtual* as a space of potentialities, distinct from the tangible, measurable world of *actual* space. Temporal techniques such as digital generative and transformational methods contain an element of the virtual: this is what allows them to give rise to unexpected results. The translation of a design from virtual to actual space is called *actualization*, and always entails discovery because the actual, by nature, is never the same as the virtual.[02] Working with virtuality produces what I call *formations*—projects that incorporate feedback from their users and environments, continuing to change even after they are built. Formations do not conform to traditional concepts of architectural type and program, as the effects and modes of occupation of such formations shift constantly.

The effects of formations produced through thermodynamic temporality and virtuality are taken up in greater detail in Chapter 04, *Affects and Effects*. *Affects* are defined as the capacity both to affect and to be affected. This distinguishes them from effects, which imply a one-way direction of causality (a cause always precedes its intended effects). In this book, we are interested not in these ordinary linear and predetermined types of effects, but in affects—unintended outcomes that have the power to cause new results and causes. In the earlier chapters of the book, I sometimes use the terms "proliferating effects," "cascading effects," or "catalytic effects" to describe affects. Affects are generated through temporal techniques that shape and transform an object, and reside in the physical features that result from these transformations: differences in form, texture, and material. These affects are activated by users,

responding to and affecting participants by affording particular capacities for use. Technological practices attempt to create *affective formations*—works that maximize their affects and generate feedback with their users and environments, potentially giving rise to larger catalytic effects.

Chapter 05, *Feed Forward: New Technologies and Future Techniques*, returns to the theme of the relationship between technologies and techniques. Instead of looking to examples from the past, however, this chapter projects forward, identifying the characteristics of technologies that may shape architectural techniques and practice in the near future. I describe how architects can recognize promising new technologies and offer a few examples drawn from the automotive, robotic manufacturing, sail manufacturing industries, as well as the material sciences.

Returning to the overall scheme of the book, the third and final trajectory is composed of samples from my work at Contemporary Architecture Practice, presented in images and short project texts. The designs and texts are intended to allow for more rapid perusal, and thus comprise a "fast" trajectory. The selected works are distributed in Chapters 02 through 05 and relate loosely to the concepts in their corresponding chapters as well as to the overall concepts of the book. The projects range widely in scale and include a Leisure Center for the 2004 Olympics in Athens, a flagship store for Reebok, a residence for a fashion designer, two high-rise towers, and a series of chaise longue chairs. All the projects are developed through temporal techniques and generate affects that are activated by their users. Thus, the reader can move back and forth between the images and descriptions of the projects and the more extensive theoretical descriptions contained in the chapter texts to gain a clearer understanding of the ideas discussed and their potential applications.

It is hoped that by providing these three distinct trajectories, or rates of flow, the book will be both cohesive and flexible enough to allow the reader to find his or her own path for negotiating the content. The aim for the book is the same as that of a catalytic formation: to instigate interactions with and innovative responses from its users.

Catalytic Formations: Architecture and Digital Design emphasizes a dynamic and interrelational approach to design that is grounded in digital techniques. Techniques enable architects to respond to new and emerging cultural contexts, and to devise methods of thinking and making that respond to our digital milieu. These techniques are formational not formal. They bring together innovations from multiple disciplines to generate catalytic formations capable of affecting and responding dynamically to users and environments. By incorporating feedback at every stage in the design process, architects can create works that fulfill architecture's potential to be a catalyst for cultural change.

01   Greg Lynn, "Architectural Curvelinearity, The Folded, the Pliant and the Supple," *Folding in Architecture*, ed. Greg Lynn (London: Architectural Design, 1993), 22–29.

02   John Rajchman, *Constructions* (Cambridge, Mass.: MIT Press, 1998), 116–117.

01 TECHNIQUES AND TECHNOLOGY

TECHNOLOGY AND FEEDBACK

Throughout history, technology and culture have formed a feedback loop: advances in technology have accelerated the pace of innovations in architecture, the arts, sciences, and media; these cultural developments have led, in turn, to new technological discoveries. The invention of iron in the eighteenth century, for example, gave rise to glass-covered arcades, "crystal palaces," and other innovative structures, which later contributed to the demand for a new technological invention: the passenger elevator. The elevator, in turn, facilitated the creation a new kind of architecture: the skyscraper, or vertical city. Similarly, at the start of the twenty-first century, digital technologies have profoundly influenced every sphere of contemporary culture, and these cultural transformations will inevitably drive the development of future technologies. In order to produce design innovation, architects cannot simply be passive recipients of technological change but, instead, must participate actively in this feedback loop between technology and culture. How can architects translate technological advances into innovative designs that produce lasting and significant cultural effects? What techniques can designers use to reinvent conventional architectural practice?

To answer these questions, I begin by unraveling the differences and relationships between often-confused terms such as *technology*, *technique*, and *technical*. The feedback loop between technology and culture is described in detail, as well as the techniques, or specific tactics, by which architects can become agents in this loop. I then enumerate the features of architecture practices that effectively use techniques to produce culturally transformative design innovation. I call such practices *technological* and offer two recent historical examples: the design practices of Charles and Ray Eames and Verner Panton. In the conclusion, I show how contemporary architecture practices can employ similar principles and techniques to pursue innovation today.

TECHNOLOGY, THE TECHNICAL, TECHNIQUE, AND FEEDBACK

A technology can be defined as the application of a purely technical or scientific advance to a cultural context. Whereas technical refinement is directed towards the efficiency of a mechanical, electrical, or digital operation, the effectiveness of a technology depends on its ability to produce in users new patterns of behavior and levels of performance. Technical efficiency is measured numerically, according to internal logics and laws; it is a value void of external meaning. Typically, the aim is greater efficiency with less material, fewer parts, and less resistance. In contrast, a technology must be judged qualitatively, by looking at how it interacts with its context and users. Technology makes the technical useful within a wider context. For example, the difference between a slower or faster modem is a matter of technical refinement. The Internet, on the other hand, is a technological advance, since it qualitatively alters the relationship between the user and the machine.

Technologies only gain meaning in their application. To be effective, new technologies require the invention of original techniques—methods that allow individuals to use technologies in specific contexts, to accomplish complex or difficult tasks. The technology of the automobile, for example, requires humans to develop techniques for driving it. Techniques are behaviors and procedures that are systematic, repeatable, and communicable. Over time and as contexts change, existing techniques may become inadequate, stimulating users to develop new methods through experimentation. For example, when confronted with a new technology such as a software program, individuals at first learn to use it through repeated practice. Later, when they have discovered the limits of the program, they may develop more advanced techniques—modulating a particular function, say, or even rewriting parts of the computer code that underlie a program. Techniques are the specific means by which architects can harness and direct the powerful potential of new technologies toward the shaping of architectural design, research, and manufacturing.

To produce further innovation, technologies and techniques must be integrated into a feedback loop—a two-way transfer of information—between a technical innovation and its context. Technical advances (such as the networking of computers) give rise to new uses or technologies (such as the Internet), leading users to create techniques (designing interactive Web sites) that, in turn, demand technical advances (faster Internet connections), which spawn new technologies (real-time three-dimensional online communities, for instance). Importantly, in each cycle of the feedback loop, the precise interaction between a technical advance and its context is unpredictable and can give rise to unexpected technological or cultural effects.

As technologies develop through multiple cycles of feedback, they often become more complex and effective, incorporating parallel functions in order to remain relevant. Over time, users develop new techniques for exploiting the technology, and the technology itself is adapted and transformed. Thus, the personal computer has evolved in the last half century from essentially a tabulation machine to one that serves simultaneously as a calculator, communications device, word processor, photo editor, and music and movie player. Each individual function contributes to the computer's expanded utility and is made possible through the machine's many redundant circuits and devices. Technological

ENIAC. University of Pennsylvania, 1941

Early computers, including the ENIAC, were application specific. Subsequent development introduced assembly language and machine language. These simple machine languages were the forerunners of the formal concept of software, which serves as a mediating technology between human beings and computers.

effectiveness evolves out of feedback with the user. The usefulness of a personal computer stems in part from its ability to fulfill a variety of functions depending on the user, application, and situation.

TECHNIQUES

Architects who seek to participate in a process of cultural change must keep abreast of developing technologies and be nimble and flexible in generating new techniques. But which technologies offer the most promise for contemporary architectural practice? How do architects develop new strategies and methods? Two possible paths exist for the evolution of new techniques: first, architects can rework existing methods within architecture—for instance, by using already available computer aided design (CAD) software in experimental ways, or even by rewriting parts of the software and adapting it to entirely new functions. Alternatively, designers may borrow techniques from other industries or fields to generate new architectural strategies—for example, importing generative techniques from the field of economic modeling to produce dynamical systems that respond to their environments, or mining the aerospace and automotive industries for new materials and construction methods.

How can architects evaluate the relative promise of new techniques for generating innovative and culturally transformative design? I suggest that they look for four principal characteristics: first, effective techniques allow the incorporation of feedback from the environment or user. Today, four-dimensional software such as Alias/Wavefront and Softimage allow designers to precisely control the parameters of techniques and to see immediately how these adjustments affect the modeling environment. Those effects can then be used to refine the technique itself. At a larger scale, within the feedback loop of technology and culture, techniques spawn effects that may give rise to new techniques, technologies, and cultural effects.

Second, new techniques destabilize existing practices. They work against equilibrium and stasis through the reinvention of standard practices. For example, Frank Gehry and Associates' use of the software CATIA on projects such as the Guggenheim Museum in Bilbao, Spain, has altered the way that buildings are designed and made. By utilizing CATIA's capacity for managing complex information in three dimensions, previously distinct parts of the building design and construction process—architectural design, mechanical, electrical and structural engineering, cost estimation, and fabrication—can now be integrated. The development of the building occurs holistically. Gehry Associates are now working to apply these innovations to change the practices of building departments across the country—advocating, for example, the acceptance of three-dimensional rather than only two-dimensional information to meet building submission requirements.

Third, techniques are process-driven. They often grow out of trial and error, evolving over time and undergoing continual adjustment until they are ultimately replaced by new techniques. For example, in the early 1990s, many architects began to investigate the transformation and differentiation of continuous surfaces. This prompted engineering firms such as Arup to develop curvature analysis software and other techniques to explore methods for structuring curvilinear forms. This research led to investigations of monocoque and semi-monocoque shells, as well as numerous other techniques. The aim of techniques should not be a final answer or solution but, instead, the development of more techniques.

Fourth, as suggested earlier, techniques are often interdisciplinary, encouraging and facilitating the transmission of expertise across areas of knowledge. For example, the software mentioned above, CATIA, was imported by Frank Gehry from the aerospace and automobile design industries. Today, a number of architects are using Maya, a software originally developed for the film industry, to generate new spatial, programmatic, and material conditions.

TECHNOLOGICAL DESIGN PRACTICES

Techniques, like architecture practices themselves, run the risk of becoming routine and static over time, no longer capable of or inclined toward innovation. For example, although technologies such as three-dimensional modeling software may have inspired innovative designs at their inception, today the use of such programs by large and small architecture practices alike has become conventional. The software are used largely for documentation and visualization, and are applied mechanically or automatically, in the same way that previous generations of architects employed drafting pens, pencils, and parallel rules. In most conventional offices, younger architects simply use CAD to implement the hand-sketched idea of a senior designer. The software merely makes this task more efficient. In this model, technology is simply collaged or superimposed onto the design process and is not allowed a more transformative role.

In contrast, I designate as "technological" those design practices that resist using technology merely to achieve efficiency. Instead,

La Chaise. Charles and Ray Eames, 1948

The Kazam. Charles and Ray Eames, 1941

Interior View. Eames House, Pacific Palisades, California. Charles and Ray Eames, 1947–49

they draw on technology to further design innovation and to propagate cultural effects. Technological design practices share several key characteristics. First, they employ techniques, as defined above—ones that incorporate feedback, are destabilizing, process-driven, and most importantly, that are interdisciplinary. The grafting of different technical and cultural lineages is a major hallmark of technological practices. Second, technological practices manufacture cultural content within a contemporary context—which today means a digital milieu. The advent of the digital age has transformed and redefined economies, social relationships, and cultural production, touching almost every sphere of the contemporary world. Techniques must be relevant to their age. Third, technological practices employ feedback from the environment into their design process rather than beginning with a preconceived design and applying it to a context. Thus, the traditional design process of concept, analysis, and construction gives way to one incorporating perpetual feedback between analysis, intervention, and exchange with the environment. Computers are not used merely as efficient tools to carry out age-old practices but, instead, their potential for generating real-time feedback and a more dynamic interactivity between design and users is tapped. Fourth, technological practices operate across different scales and contexts—from the molecular scale of materials to the scale of the body, from the dimensions of a building to those of the city. Their strategies and operations can be conceived as scaleless—equally applicable to many situations. Details are retained in their work from the largest to the smallest scale. Fifth, technological practices generate techniques and projects that instigate proliferating effects on the wider culture and society. They are *catalytic*, generating positive feedback, intelligence, and adaptation across multiple disciplines and fields of design knowledge.

THE EAMESES: AN OMNIVOROUS TECHNOLOGICAL PRACTICE

A clearer understanding of how technological practices manifest these criteria can be gained by looking at two examples from recent history: the work of the American architects Charles and Ray Eames and the Danish furniture and interior designer Verner Panton. Both sets of designers employed a range of techniques grounded in their contemporary milieus. Both the Eameses and Panton undertook projects of multiple scales that generated larger cultural effects. And both worked iteratively, incorporating successive cycles of feedback into their projects.

The design and architecture team of Charles and Ray Eames adapted the technical advancements made during World War II to develop some of the most sophisticated techniques of their time. Their practice was omnivorous, drawing on innovations from disciplines ranging from the automotive industry to boat building to the material sciences to the nascent field of computer science. In some instances, the Eameses combined advances from these disciplines with their own inventions to generate entirely new technologies and techniques. In the early 1940s, for example, as part of their explorations into inexpensive plywood molding methods, they created a device called the Kazam by combining various existing technologies such as a bicycle pump, electrical heater, plaster mold, and rubber tire membrane. The homemade machine pressed heated plywood against a plaster mold. Multiple layers of wood were then laminated together using glue technology that Charles learned about as a set designer at MGM Studios. The Eameses developed several techniques for using the Kazam, learning as they went and incorporating feedback from the process to continually refine their techniques. The Kazam was used first to produce a plywood leg splint and later several iterations of their pioneering curved plywood chair.

The Eameses were deeply interested in engaging with the contemporary economic and cultural conditions of their time—the age of mechanical mass production. While a student at Cranbrook Academy of the Arts, Charles had become fascinated with the mass production process used by Ford and other automobile manufacturers and had studied Albert Kahn's designs for prefabricated Ford automobile plants. From the Chrysler Motorcar Company, the Eameses learned about a technique of high frequency electronic welding, which they imported to secure rubber shock mounts to their plywood chairs, enabling the mounting of metal legs to the chairs without visible screws or fasteners. They not only adapted techniques from industrial mass production, but through the furniture company Herman Miller, were able to effectively mass produce many of their own furniture designs for a broad audience.

Ever restless in their search for new techniques and materials, the Eameses became interested, in the late 1940s, in creating curved chairs out of fiberglass. Initially, each chair was made individually: the fiberglass was layered by hand using a technique borrowed from the glass fabric and resin manufacturing industry, and each chair was finished by hand. Later, the couple worked with Zenith Plastics, a firm that had made plastic radar domes during World War II, to mass produce the chairs at an affordable cost to consumers. These investigations fulfilled the Eameses' ambition to engage in contemporary practices of mass production.[01]

The Eameses applied the techniques developed in their furniture designs to all scales of their work, including architecture. In 1949, they built a house in Los Angeles as part of the Case Study Houses program sponsored by the magazine *Art and Architecture*. Even at this larger scale, they again tried to apply techniques of mechanized mass production, this time in the pursuit of methods to alleviate the projected postwar housing shortage in the US.[02] The Eames House, as it became known, used prefabricated, standardized parts and industrial materials, including steel trusses, fiberglass panels, plywood, and a repetitive and standardized window sash. Built out of products available through mail order catalogs, the entire structure of the house was erected in a day and a half.

The Eameses were always interested in updating their techniques and persistently explored new technological trajectories as they became available. They worked within existing conditions but ceaselessly forged toward the future through their innovations. Thus, even while they were engaged in developing mechanical mass production techniques to manufacture furniture and architecture, they looked ahead to the possibilities engendered by another newly emerging technology—the computer. During the 1960s, the Eameses became increasingly interested in the potential of computation—specifically in the interactivity between machines and users and in the computer's capacity to communicate scientific advancements in legible and interesting ways. They created several exhibition designs for IBM that brought together their interests in film and computation. Their exhibition *Think*, sponsored by IBM for the 1964 World's Fair in New York, featured multiple projection screens arrayed at various heights and angles, set before a "People Wall" of 400 viewers seated in a raised elliptical theater. The multiscreen, multimedia program demonstrated the latest computer technologies and also sought to produce new cultural effects. In the Eameses' multimedia installation, the actor was completely absent; instead, the screened documentary film itself became the environment. Their exhibit anticipated later developments in digital interactivity and performance theater. The Eameses adapted to and embraced the new horizons introduced by digital technologies. They presciently foresaw in computers the future of cultural evolution. While the Eameses' practice is exemplary for its individual

S-Stuhl, Model 276. Verner Panton, 1960

Stacking Chair Prototype. Verner Panton, 1960

Stacking Chair, later known as the Panton Chair. Verner Panton, 1967

innovations, it is even more notable for the foresight, breadth, and interdisciplinarity of its techniques.

The Eameses' design practice produced widespread cultural effects—some planned and others unexpected. Although their furnishings eventually became nearly ubiquitous, especially in institutions such as schools and offices, at first, some of the fiberglass chair designs provoked mild alarm among the public: many people were afraid to sit on them because they looked "too thin." The synthetic material and complex molded forms of the chairs made them surprisingly strong, but they did not align with contemporary sensibilities regarding stability. The pieces contradicted expectations about the appropriate volume and massing of furniture. The couple set the stage for countless later designers, including Verner Panton, to create similarly counterintuitive and light designs. As one leading newspaper put it, Charles Eames "changed the way the twentieth century sat down."[03] A further effect of the Eameses' work was the adoption by the fiberglass industry of techniques for the mass production of furniture. Today, many products made of variations of these composite materials are produced at all scales.

VERNER PANTON: A RESEARCH-BASED TECHNOLOGICAL PRACTICE

Like the Eameses, the Danish architect and designer Verner Panton appropriated techniques from a range of other disciplines to cultivate a technological design practice. From the material sciences, he gleaned techniques for working with plastics, a category of materials that had existed since the late nineteenth century, but only became available on a larger scale for non-industrial uses in the 1950s. Plastics provided Panton with a unique canvas to explore his interests in color and Pop Art, and eventually led him to investigate techniques of mass production and molding developed by the automobile industry.

Panton's techniques and designs continually evolved through experimentation and feedback. In 1956, Panton had developed a stackable, cantilevered plywood chair for the WK European Furniture Design Competition. His knowledge of the techniques and limitations of working with plywood prompted him to look for a material that was lighter and stronger, a search that led him to plastics. In 1951, scientists at Phillips Petroleum researching chemical additives for gasoline accidentally invented crystalline polypropylene and high-density polyethylene (HDPE) plastic—also known by the trade name Marlex®—a more pliable and less brittle version of the material than those previously available. Panton capitalized on this discovery, and began experimenting with the potential forms of the new material.

In 1960, he developed a prototype of a cantilevered chair made of extruded polystyrene, which he refined and developed through ten iterations between 1960 and 1963.[04] By 1966, Panton began collaborating with the Herman Miller Company and Vitra to develop the chair in different materials.[05] A version of the fiberglass chair was manufactured using a mechanized cold-press fiberglass-reinforced polyester resin in 1967, but the molded chairs were extremely heavy and had to be sanded and finished by hand. Panton was interested in using mass production methods to exploit the potentials of plastic. A lighter polyurethane foam version of the chair was developed the following year, but it still required hand finishing. In spite of this, the chairs could be produced relatively rapidly, at a rate of one chair every thirty minutes, including the lacquering process. Panton wanted to offer the chair in as many colors as possible, and it eventually became available in seven different lacquer hues.

The design of the Panton Chair, as it became known, evolved not only in response to Panton's design directives, but also through successive cycles of feedback with advancing technologies. The form of the chair changed as new materials became available. Early versions were heavy and the curves bulbous and awkward. As Panton's knowledge of the material and access to recent developments in plastics research grew, the chair's design progressed. By 1971, an injection-molded thermoplastic version of the chair exhibited the smooth curvilinear surface familiar today as well as structural ribs inside the base that provided stability. Later, in 1983, when polyurethane foam became available, it was immediately used by Panton to produce a lighter iteration, which led to the introduction in 1990 of a mass-produced injection-molded edition in a scratch-resistant matte finish.[06] The Panton Chair was the first monolithic plastic chair and ushered forth many subsequent developments in plastics-based industrial design.

Panton extended his exploration of plastics and foam to larger scales in his designs for integrated furniture and interior environments. These projects allowed the designer to further his explorations of form, color, lighting, and materials such as fiberglass, plastics, steel, foam rubber, and other synthetics. By creating environments that manipulated the body's relationship to space, Panton wanted to investigate the capacity of different spatial arrangements to engender new social organizations. Integrated furniture pieces such as the Living Tower (1968) and Pantower (1969) featured seating at various heights and positions, providing the user with myriad modes of engagement and a new understanding of the surrounding space.[07] In his

experimental interior landscapes and environments, such as Visiona II (1970), an exhibition space sponsored by the Bayer chemical company, Panton proposed a vision of a "fantasy landscape" for the future home. The designer hoped to encourage users to fantasize about different ways of using their living spaces. Concentrating on the idea of leisure space, he conceived an interior environment made of curvilinear fluid pieces. The design reflected his interest in overcoming the traditional divisions of a room into walls, floors, and ceilings in favor of a single unified design that would be open to different uses and situations. The environment would inflect and alter the human body and its relationship to the furnishings and interiors, in addition to stimulating new groupings and forms of interaction between users.

CONTEMPORARY TECHNOLOGICAL PRACTICES

Both the Eameses and Panton developed innovative techniques to apply new technologies to their cultural contexts. Today, the essential attributes of technological practices remain fundamentally the same, even if the contexts have changed. Just as an earlier generation of designers sought to grapple with the social, cultural, and economic realities of the era of mass production, today's architects must fully engage the conditions and possibilities of the digital age. Like their predecessors, contemporary technological practices must import inventions from other disciplines to develop new techniques. For example, designers might adopt modeling software from the automobile and aeronautics industries that offer new techniques for creating surface geometries, or innovations from the field of robotics that might be applied to enable the three-dimensional "printing" of an entire house. By drawing on innovations from other fields, architects can tap the power of the digital to create dynamic testing environments and produce more precise manufacturing methods. These effects may feed forward to the development of additional techniques that further inflect and contribute to the development of architecture.

Contemporary technological practices also must use feedback to continually reshape techniques and technologies. Once again, we can look at the example of Frank Gehry Associates' use of CATIA. After successfully applying CATIA to integrate the design and

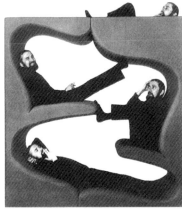

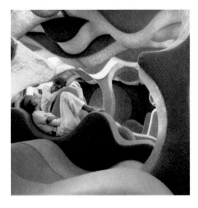

Cold-Press Mold. Verner Panton, 1967
Living Tower. Verner Panton, 1969
Visiona II. Verner Panton, 1970

construction processes for the Guggenheim Museum in Bilbao, Gehry formed a separate consultancy firm, Gehry Technologies, to further develop the software's potential architectural uses. Dassault Systems, the creator of CATIA, joined with IBM to fund Gehry Technologies' work on refining the software in four specific areas: formal design, curvature analysis, integration of engineering and other building systems, and manufacturing. This partnership has given rise to other effects: a new version of CATIA that can run on the widely used Windows platform will allow exponentially more firms and designers to use the software. As increasing numbers of fabricators acquire and learn to use CATIA, the building industry's long-entrenched modes of operation may gradually be transformed, resulting in yet unknown new forms of architecture that may enable new forms of interactivity between design and users.

Contemporary technological practices employ scaleless techniques that can be applied equally well to the design of products and cities. Zaha Hadid, for example, uses similar digital methods to design and manufacture a tea set for Donna Karan, furniture for Vitra, an installation for a museum in Vienna, and the Headquarters for the BMW Motorcar Company in Leipzig, Germany. Her design research and concerns maintain a continuity and coherence, although the specific pressures and relationships at play change in response to the local parameters of each project. The ability to use the digital at every stage of an architectural project from conception to fabrication allows for contemporary technological practices to seamlessly operate between scales, preserving complexity through all levels of design.

Within architecture, the invention of new techniques alters the shape of the design product, producing effects on human behavior and inhabitation. This feedback loop between techniques, forms, and users can be seen in Foreign Office Architects' Ferry Port Terminal project (2002) in Yokohama, Japan. The architects used techniques from roller coaster design to engineer the complex curves and intersecting surfaces of the building. During the development of the design, the transformation of one part of the continuous surface inflected the whole of the project—as it would in a roller coaster. This unique design process resulted in a series of complex spaces and areas which, in their built form, inspire unexpected behaviors and uses. At the intersections of curvilinear walls, niches are created: these provide shelter to travelers who wish to lie down. On the flatter, exposed surfaces of the building, children have been known to spontaneously dance or families to picnic. These actions instigate responses by other users: an entire area may temporarily become a lounge, stage, or picnic ground, affecting the provisional uses of adjacent spaces. A shift in one area inflects the whole. Thus, behaviors and patterns of use emerge that reflect the very techniques used to create the building. The techniques catalyze architectural forms that lead to proliferating effects on modes of inhabitation and use.

Technological practices develop techniques that relate to a particular cultural moment and context. Such techniques open architecture to a feedback loop incorporating cultural and technological developments from outside the discipline and resulting in buildings with innovative formal, spatial, and material outcomes. These architectural spaces, in turn, produce effects that influence human behaviors—effects that may lead to the development of new techniques and technologies. By employing techniques, contemporary technological practices seek to engage in a feedback loop that yields catalytic cultural effects.

01   Pat Kirkham, *Charles and Ray Eames: Designers of the Twentieth Century* (Cambridge, Mass.: MIT Press, 1995), 209.

02   John Neuhart, Marilyn Neuhart, and Ray Eames, *Eames Design: The Work of the Offices of Charles and Ray Eames* (New York: Abrams, 1989), 22.

03   Quoted in Donald Albrecht, "Introduction," in *The Work of Charles and Ray Eames: A Legacy of Invention* (New York: Abrams, 1997), 15.

04   "Verner Panton Resource Pack" (London: Design Museum, 2001), 12.

05   Ibid., 4.

06   "Verner Panton," in *A Century of Chairs* (London: Design Museum, 2003). (Online: http://www.designmuseum.org.uk/designerex/verner-panton.htm)

07   Alexander von Vegesack and Mathias Remmele, *Verner Panton: The Collected Works* (Weil-am-Rhein, Germany: Vitra Design Museum, 2000), 67.

02 TEMPORALITY AND TIME

Architecture traditionally has been associated with notions of permanence and stability—in short, with the negation of time and its consequences. Most architects, if they think about time at all, see its effects as something to be resisted. In this chapter, I argue that technological design practices—which I define in Chapter 01 as those that use techniques and technology to produce design innovation—must take a radically different approach to time and temporality. Far from being the foe of architects, time can be an ally in the production of transformative design.

To understand how technological practices can integrate temporality into their modes of operation and how this departs from the way conventional practices regard time, it is necessary to understand the differences between two models of time from the sciences. The divergence between these two theories of temporality will be shown to underlie some crucial distinctions between conventional and technological architecture practices. In the sections below, I begin by sketching the theoretical underpinnings of temporality in architecture. I then discuss the main ways that these concepts of time influence technological and conventional practices—that is, in the nature of their evolution over time, their aims, and techniques. I argue that technological practices use what I call *temporal techniques* to create innovative works of architecture, and offer three examples of architects who use such techniques.

THEORIES OF TEMPORALITY AND TIME

Within the sciences, it is possible to distinguish between two theories of time and temporality—one based on physics and classical mechanics and the other based on thermodynamics. In the first model of temporality, time is essentially a neutral container for events occurring in it.[01] Time is "reversible." This does not mean that it can flow backwards, but rather, that for any given process that occurs over time, the fundamental properties of the materials involved do not change.[02] In other words, if one were to record an event—a ball being thrown upwards in the air, for example—and then play it in reverse, the fundamental properties of the event would not change, only the direction.[03] In such a world, time is reduced to its numerical aspect: it is conceived as series of static points or numbers on a line, and past and future are, in a sense, symmetrical. Events are predictable and stable, since one can move backwards or forwards in time and see no transformation in the basic properties of objects. Finally, time and any changes that occur in time can be reduced to their quantitative aspects: the time it takes for the ball to reach the height of its arc, for example, or the distance it travels.

In thermodynamics, on the other hand, most processes are "irreversible," meaning there is a fundamental asymmetry between past and future. For example, ice melts into water but playing this event in reverse produces the opposite process: freezing rather than melting. The basic properties of the material, water, have been radically altered; it has changed qualitatively over time. Thus, thermodynamic temporality incorporates both quantitative and qualitative change, or the prospect that something can change in kind not just in number. Thermodynamic temporality includes the numerical component of time, and adds to it a potential for qualitative change—what I will define later in this book as the *virtual*. These two aspects—the numerical and the

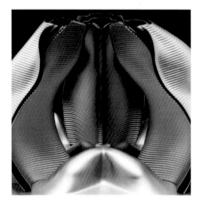

Fabricated Variation Studies. Alessi Tea and Coffee Set. Greg Lynn FORM, 2000–03

Alessi Tea and Coffee Set. Greg Lynn FORM, 2000–03

Alessi Tea and Coffee Set. Greg Lynn FORM, 2000–03

virtual—give thermodynamic temporality its generative potential. And it is this possibility of creating something new that is of interest to technological practices.

TEMPORALITY AND THE ORGANIZATION OF PRACTICE

Whether consciously or not, all architecture practices operate according to an implicit theory of time. Most conventional offices can be said to follow the first model of temporality, whereby time is essentially a neutral container in which to carry out established procedures. The development of these practices is "reversible"—meaning that they tend not to undergo changes "in kind"; their fundamental properties generally remain constant. Firms can add a few employees and later subtract them but they operate in essentially the same way, relying on standard forms of organization, design methodologies, and representational techniques. The parallel rule may have given way to the computer, but this still has not altered how these offices design architecture.

Technological practices also operate according to this numerical model of time but, in addition, feature several characteristics that incorporate thermodynamic temporality. For example, rather than conceiving of themselves as static entities, technological practices regard themselves as momentary configurations that transform over time. Their shapes, forms, and organization change as they reinvent themselves and their techniques in response to shifting contexts. The developmental paths of technological practices are "irreversible," meaning they undergo transformations in kind that make them fundamentally different from moment to moment.

For an example of constant reinvention, we can look at the practice of Greg Lynn FORM. In the late 1990s, Lynn pioneered a number of computer-based techniques for working with curvilinear surfaces—for example, Blebs and lattice modeling. These techniques helped to define FORM as a "paperless" office, one focused on the digital realm. However, Lynn subsequently became interested in a new technology, the computer numerically controlled (CNC) milling machine. In developing techniques to use this new fabrication device, Lynn's practice shifted its focus to become a testing ground for the fabrication of installations and buildings. Materials and their transformation through pressure have become central concerns of the practice. Techniques developed through experimenting with fabrication and materials differ from ones generated within the computer. As its techniques have shifted, Lynn's practice has transformed irreversibly.

Another way that divergent theories of temporality inform conventional and technological practices differently is in their aims. Here again, conventional practices can be understood as implicitly following the model of temporality developed by physics, with its emphasis on the numerical aspects of change. Conventional architecture firms tend to measure progress quantitatively—in terms of size of projects, efficiency, and profit. To maximize these ends, offices employ techniques such as libraries of detail drawings that can be reused on multiple projects. Such techniques not only serve to maintain the stasis, predictability, and hence reversibility of the work produced, but also preclude new effects and techniques from emerging. In contrast, technological practices are concerned with both the quantitative and qualitative aspects of change over time—in other words, those facets encompassed by both kinds of temporality. They aim to produce techniques and works of architecture that are different in kind and not just in their quantifiable, measurable dimensions. For example, technological practices are interested in software that allows them to integrate engineering, formmaking, and other aspects of the design process—not for the sake of greater efficiency, but to expand the potentials for collaboration and cross-fertilization between these areas. Such techniques open new possibilities for innovative designs.

TEMPORALITY AND TECHNIQUES

Whereas conventional offices carry out techniques in the neutral container of time that tend to result in predictable, static objects, technological practices employ what I call *temporal techniques*, which yield objects that continue to change even after they are built. Before delving into the details of what constitute temporal techniques, it is worthwhile perhaps to review the working processes of conventional architecture practices, in order to understand how they differ from the methods being advocated here. Most offices work through a sequence of design, analysis, representation, and building: architects come up with an overarching concept or design; proceed to analyze the structure, uses, functionality, mechanical systems, cost, and myriad other conditions; represent the design in progressively more detailed drawings and renderings; and then build it according to the representations. After the initial generation of the concept, however, at each subsequent stage of the process, the end result is largely known. Various techniques are employed to make the structure more efficient, say, or to rearrange rooms in a more functional manner, but none of these techniques substantively changes the initial concept. In fact, every effort is made not to change the initial design—in order to preserve the "clarity" of the concept.

Consequently, the techniques used are ones that achieve their ends (typically, quantitatively measurable ones) but nothing more. Techniques do not lead to unexpected effects or to the generation of new techniques and design research. Instead, similar to the example of the ball that is thrown up in the air, this process of design is as predictable as the arc of the ball. I call such design processes *analytical*. In contrast, temporal techniques incorporate both forms of temporality, allowing the architect to alter both the quantitatively measurable and the qualitative aspects of a design. Because they produce changes in kind, not just number, such techniques render the design process irreversible. In other words, at no point in the process is the final result known; on the contrary, the hope is that the techniques, used intelligently, will generate unanticipated catalytic effects.

Temporal techniques share several characteristics. First, they synthesize the normative analytical methods used by conventional practices with bottom-up approaches. Architects who use analytical methods typically work from the top down: they formulate an overall design concept and then refine the design at successively more detailed levels. Designers who use temporal techniques begin, instead, with the individual parts of a system, linking these elements together to form larger components until a complete assemblage emerges. Each step in the process reshapes and redirects the next. Hence, new associations and outcomes may arise that were not anticipated. Designers then evaluate these bottom-up procedures analytically, to determine whether the aims of the project are fulfilled or to make sure it can be built efficiently. Bottom-up methods supplement rather than supplant analysis. The emphasis shifts, however, from trying to analyze or represent that which is already known—the preconceived design concept—to discovering relationships and techniques that are not yet known and that may emerge through feedback.

Second, temporal techniques are nonlinear. They do not proceed through simple, or linear, cause and effect. Nonlinear techniques combine existing entities in such a way that they produce new and emergent organizations that are more than the sum of their parts. These new formations are irreducible—just as the liquidity of water cannot be divided into the individual properties of the hydrogen or oxygen atoms that compose it, nor a tornado to the winds that precede it. Rather than composing a building by

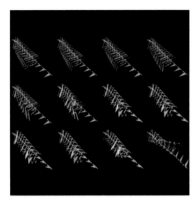

Inverse Kinematic (IK) Chains with Attached Surface. H2 House, Schwechat, Austria. Greg Lynn FORM, 1996

H2 House, Schwechat, Austria. Greg Lynn FORM, 1996

Site Plan Detail. 1,050 Pre-Fabricated Houses, Eindhoven, the Netherlands. Lars Spuybroek, NOX, 1998

adding together blocks of program, nonlinear techniques strive to generate a whole that exceeds its individual components, yielding unexpected forms, materials, and modes of inhabiting space. The behavior of nonlinear systems is difficult to predict. To understand and manipulate the performance of a nonlinear system, one must study it as a whole as well as its components.

Third, temporal techniques combine numerical and *virtual* components. Because the concept of the virtual is such a complex and important subject, it will be discussed more fully in Chapter 03 and its role in temporal techniques will be glossed over in the examples below. For now, the crucial point is that temporal techniques include both factors that the designer controls numerically and ones that emerge in unforseeable ways from the interactions of the system's parts. These unpredictable possibilities constitute the technique's virtual element.

In this chapter, I focus specifically on two families of temporal techniques: *generative* and *transformational* techniques. Generative techniques use algorithms written into computer code to determine the state of a system at an incremental point in the future. As the algorithm is repeated iteratively, the system evolves over time. With each incremental step, the system is irreversibly changed. Transformational techniques use digital software to manipulate continuous surfaces—objects structured in such a way that manipulating any point on the surface causes all other points to be redistributed. Applying transformational operations such as folding, stretching, cutting, and pressuring to these continuous surfaces results in changes to the whole. However, because the effects of the transformation are distributed, the precise outcome of an operation cannot always be predicted in advance. Transformational techniques thus are also irreversible, producing changes in kind not just in number.

GENERATIVE TECHNIQUES: HYDROGEN HOUSE AND 1,050 PREFABRICATED HOUSES

Generative techniques draw on several software packages borrowed from the automotive and film industries. These programs—Alias/Wavefront and Softimage, for example—permit designers to create and work with dynamical systems and thermodynamic temporality. For some examples of how technological practices use dynamical systems as part of their design processes, we can look at two projects by Greg Lynn FORM and Lars Spuybroek of NOX. Both practices use generative temporal techniques to create innovative buildings with potentially significant cultural effects.

In designing the Hydrogen House (1996), a multifunctional visitor and demonstration center for hydrogen in Schwechat, Austria, Greg Lynn combined traditional analytical methods with bottom-up temporal techniques. Lynn began by studying two key relationships on the site: the center's connection to an adjacent high-speed road and the requirement that the building generate its own power from the environment—specifically, through the collection of solar energy by photovoltaic panels. The designer created a dynamical system using the software Alias/Wavefront. Into this system, he imported information about the path of the sun through four seasons and the speed of vehicles moving past the site. Lynn attached the trajectories of the sun and vehicles to pressure fields and defined the way that these pressure fields interacted. As the sun and vehicles moved, their pressure fields combined to create turbulence. The designer then generated a set of geometries called inverse-kinematic (IK) chains, which consist of parts connected like bones in a skeletal system. The bones were covered with a "skin" or surface. Next, Lynn applied the pressure fields generated by the sun and traffic movements to his geometric system, precisely defining the parameters governing the relationships between environmental pressures and the geometry. At first, the pressure fields were too strong and essentially blew apart the IK chains. So Lynn repeatedly modulated the constraints controlling the interaction between pressure field and geometry until a more productive relationship developed—or, put another way, until feedback emerged between the environment and the architecture. Lynn worked from the bottom up, manipulating the individual components of the pressures and IK chains and their mutual relationships through trial and error. After each iteration, he applied analytical methods to evaluate the performance of the dynamical system and to determine the next step. Although each relationship in the system—between sun and pressure field, between pressure field and geometrical structure, between the individual bones of the geometry, and between bones and skin—was precisely defined, together they generated movements and outcomes that were nonlinear—that were more than the sum of their parts. Unexpected configurations and movements emerged.

In the Hydrogen House, these temporal techniques are legible in the building itself, manifesting themselves in a heterogeneous range of surface inflections. The building envelope is a continuous whole that features different attributes without being reducible to its parts. In other words, it is a nonlinear system. The surface that receives the most exposure to the sun's trajectories, the south facade, is inflected to maximize the collection of sunlight by photovoltaic panels attached to the envelope. This energy is used to generate electricity for the building and its exhibits, allowing the building to literally feed off its environment. On the side of the museum facing the road, a series

of cuts and twists in the building envelope allows passing motorists glimpses into the exhibitions inside. Other outcomes, perhaps unanticipated, also develop: for instance, the architectural envelope becomes entwined with the exhibition surfaces, challenging the traditional concept of the exhibition space as a simple white box.

Another designer who uses computer-based dynamical systems is Lars Spuybroek, principal of the firm NOX. For 1,050 Prefabricated Houses (1998), a residential development located in Eindhoven, the Netherlands, Spuybroek used generative temporal techniques to approach several scales of the project simultaneously—from the overall master plan to the shape of each individual housing unit. Spuybroek began by inventing a technique in Alias/Wavefront based on elasticity. In the computer, he modeled a series of 100 elastic lines that stretched across the site, perpendicular to a four-lane road that bisected the area. The designer defined the parameters of the dynamical system by assigning directions and velocities to the central highway and surrounding thoroughfares, based on actual site conditions. In addition, he attached the elastic lines to springs, and gave the springs properties of influence over adjacent springs. Modulating these numerically controlled parameters gave rise to nonlinear effects: over time, the two sets of dynamically changing pressures—one from the roads and the other between the springs themselves—combined to generate a variable pressure field. Pressure gradients formed in the field, deforming the shape and position of the springs.

The first time Spuybroek tested this system, the springs moved but did not develop any cohesive behaviors. He then analyzed the results and adjusted the parameters of the system until positive feedback between the system of elastic lines and the environment emerged. The result was a moiré pattern of different densities—a nonlinear outcome, since it was a new organization that could not be reduced to its components. The variation in densities determined the placement of housing units on the site as well as the degree of transformation—specifically, the rotation and bending point—of each house. A similar process was repeated at the scale of the housing unit. Instead of being shaped by traffic patterns, however, the geometry of each individual house responded to pressures associated with domestic activities of

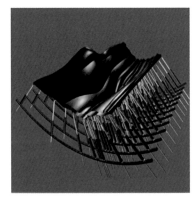

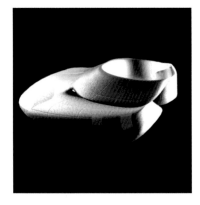

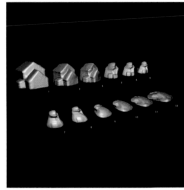

Detailed Transformations of Individual House. 1,050 Pre-Fabricated Houses, Eindhoven, the Netherlands. Lars Spuybroek, NOX, 1998

Transformation between Originator and Target. Housings. KOL/MAC Studio, 1999

First Set of Exterior Transformations. Housings. KOL/MAC Studio, 1999

varying intensities: high-intensity undertakings such as parking the car and entertaining, medium-intensity occupations such as bathing and cooking, and low-intensity pursuits such as reading and relaxing. These pressures dynamically inflected the shape of each house, resulting in dwellings that eschewed traditional boundaries between domestic spaces and that potentially would alter their users' lifestyles. In addition, at the scale of the master plan, arranging the houses in response to traffic pressures rather than in a more conventional subdivision organization inspired a rethinking of traditional site planning concepts.

Each stage of Spuybroek's design process used the previous step as its starting point. He did not begin with a preconceived design; instead, the form emerged from the process. He worked from the bottom up, but applied analytical tools of evaluation at each stage. His techniques were generative and operated on the implicit assumption of irreversible—that is, thermodynamic—temporality. Feedback within the process between project and environment led to the architecture's catalytic potential.

TRANSFORMATIONAL TECHNIQUES: HOUSINGS

Whereas Lynn and Spuybroek both employ generative techniques to determine the shape of a system incrementally in time, the architects Sulan Kolatan and William MacDonald (KOL/MAC) use another category of temporal procedures to design architecture. These are what I call transformational techniques: processes that change a material irreversibly in time, leading to unexpected effects. For their project Housings (1999), a series of six prefabricated houses, all based on the typology of a two-and-a-half bathroom colonial-style house, KOL/MAC Studio invented a transformational technique called "shape-shifting." The designers used the software Alias/Wavefront to alter the geometry of a meta-object in a digital environment.[04] A meta-object is a sphere with two zones of influence, an inner and an outer zone. When two meta-objects are placed next to one another, their zones of influence mutually stretch and deform each other's surfaces. If the influences are strong enough, they may even fuse into one meta-object. The relationships between meta-objects can be manipulated by adjusting their numeric parameters, such as the strength and propensies of their zones of influence.

In Housings, KOL/MAC Studio used the colonial house as one meta-object, and applied a series of shape-shifting transformations to fuse it with a variety of other meta-objects—primarily objects from industrial design. The colonial house was the "originator" and the industrial design objects were "targets." After the first series of transformations, which focused on the exterior of the building, the architects analyzed the results according to specific performance criteria: for example, suitability for various human activities and correspondence with the landscape. The transformations yielded what Kolatan and MacDonald termed "monsters," "noise," and "supremes." A monster was an absurd enlargement and contortion of a single area, noise referred to intersecting surfaces and unrecognizable distortions to the form, and a supreme was any transformation not included in the first two categories. A second series of transformations was performed, focused on the house's interior space; these aimed at shape-shifting supremes with programmatically specific targets such as bathtubs, sinks, and benches. The architects worked from the bottom up, beginning with components of the design but no preconceived idea of the end. They worked iteratively, analyzing the process at every step to determine whether the results of their transformations met their goals for the project, and readjusting their techniques accordingly.

Kolatan and MacDonald's transformational techniques produced hybridized houses with innovative forms, combinations of material, and living spaces. The effects of these innovations on lifestyles, concepts of domesticity, and the relationship between architecture and industrial product design are yet to be seen. Because the end product emerged from a series of transformations, each one dependent on the one before it, the process was irreversible. Small changes in an earlier step often led to unpredictable variations. The results of KOL/MAC Studio's techniques were nonlinear: although the initial parameters could be numerically controlled, they led to outcomes that exceeded the sum of their parts.

The techniques cited above constitute only a small sampling of the wide range of temporal techniques available to technological practices. Such techniques incorporate characteristics of thermodynamic temporality such as irreversibility and the potential for generating new conditions. They incorporate bottom-up and nonlinear processes with more traditional analytical methods. Using temporal techniques allows technological practices to produce works that differ radically from the buildings generated by conventional practices using more standard methods. Operating according to thermodynamic temporality also leads practices to think of themselves less as static entities and more as momentary coalescences of collaborators, interests, and techniques. The aims of such practices are expanded from merely quantitative objectives, such as efficiency, to include the goal of generating qualitatively new forms of architecture. By conceiving of time and change as irreversible phenomena that open the way for unexpected effects and outcomes, architects can alter their working methods and the potency of their designs. A static conception of time results in static buildings. Working with thermodynamic temporality, on the other hand, enables architects to produce catalytic works of architecture, ones that feed forward to the further development of new architectural techniques and possibilities.

PROJECT 01 PERFORMATIVE LEISURES

Leisure Center for the 2004 Olympic Games
Athens, Greece, 2002–03

The Leisure Center is intended to serve athletes and visitors at
the 2004 Olympic Games in Athens, Greece. The site of the
30,000-square-foot project is south of the city, directly opposite
the Hellenike Olympic Complex, which contains the venues for
basketball, baseball, canoe and kayak, and hockey. The main
goals of the project are twofold: first, to provide a space for
relaxation and recreation both during and after the Olympic
Games and, second, to catalyze interactions and cultural
exchanges between local users and tourists and between the
center and its users.

The project was developed through a bottom-up process that
combined research, analysis, and experimentation in dynamical
system techniques. The first step was to study and compare
leisure activities around the world. We found that there were four
general categories of leisure activity practiced worldwide:
domestic (such as cooking and gardening), cultural (going to the
theater or movies), social (congregating with friends or in
organized clubs), and recreational (such as sports, reading, and
painting). Preferences for each type of leisure activity varied by
continent: for example, cultural activities were popular in Europe
but less popular in Africa; social activities were prevalent in Asia
but less common in North America.

This research was then brought into the computer. Using the
program Maya, we created a dynamical system model composed
of pressures correlated to the four categories of leisure activities.
The pressures were interconnected with springs in order to
maximize the interaction between the leisure activities. The
pressures were given equal intensities except for social leisure,
which was given more weight in deference to local Greek
preferences for activities such as having a coffee, eating out, and
meeting friends. In addition, various site-related factors and the
building itself were assigned pressures so that they would exert
a force on the leisure activities contained within the center.
Feedback developed between the internal pressures of the leisure
programs and external site-related pressures, creating trajectories
of different speeds. This pressure system was then applied to a
field of particles. The software allowed us to specify the behavior

of each particle, including its tendencies to avoid collisions, split, merge, and spawn new particles. When activated by the pressures, each particle influenced and was influenced by adjacent particles, generating affects within the system. Through the careful modulation of the pressure system and particle behaviors, feedback developed, and distinct patterns of linear accumulations emerged in the system.

The dynamical system was then actualized[05] in metric space by using the particles as control points to produce spline-based geometries and surfaces. The movement of each particle was traced over a period of time to generate a three-dimensional curve or spline. These splines were connected to form the project's various stretched and inverted surfaces. Affects[06] were contained in areas inflected with the most intense transformations, as indicated by the density of particles. Low-density accumulations of particles generated inhabitable surfaces, linear bundles became circulation paths connecting the inhabitable surfaces, and clusters gave rise to openings connecting the floor and roof surfaces. Materials and construction methods were specified: the center would be made of a prefabricated aluminum structure and formwork and lightweight concrete cast on site.

In developing the formation, we adjusted our techniques to maximize affects, or areas that would have the most potential to affect users. Some spaces are assigned provisional uses, such as the bar and café. Areas with a greater range of surface inflections contain more affects. These zones have the potential to giver rise to a larger range of functions and therefore are left indeterminate. Boundaries between program areas are indistinct, allowing users a degree of ambiguity in moving between different activities and creating the possibility that leisure activities will be hybridized. The uses of the undefined areas change as they are occupied. Unforeseen relationships may emerge as visitors of different nationalities and ages interact with the center's spaces and activate its various affects and affordances.[07] Each user has his or her own affects— shaped by age, size, and cultural background—that influence how he or she interacts with the affordances of the formation. A series of steps may provide some a place to sunbathe and relax and others a space to sit and watch a movie. Users influence those around them, affecting the way that groups form and interact with the surface. Thus, the abstraction and indeterminacy of the center's forms instigate intercultural exchanges based not on symbolism or iconography but on the interactions of bodies in space. Context also plays a role: on pleasant days, users may gather on the steps while on especially hot days they may disperse into the formation's shade-covered areas. The center's uses may spill outside, blurring the boundary between building and landscape. Movement into and out of the formation activates affects in the center's glass doors, which pivot to allow a continuous transition between interior and exterior.

The center permits many leisure spaces to occur simultaneously, maximizing the possibility that unforeseen relationships will emerge through the feedback between users, the inhabitable surfaces of the building, and the context. Instead of specifying a post-Olympics program for the center, it is hoped that the formation's indeterminacy will allow it to continue to be useful—with the understanding that usefulness is an emergent condition that changes as the formation's affects are activated differently by distinct users. Most importantly for the mission of the Olympics, the center shifts the emphasis from symbolic expressions of race, color, and nationality to the unpredictable relationships that emerge as bodies interact within an affective space.

Dynamical Systems with Springs and Particle Fields

Dynamical System with Springs Mapped through Time

A   Trajectory
B   Particle Clusters
C   Low Density Accumulation of Particles
D   Linear Bundles

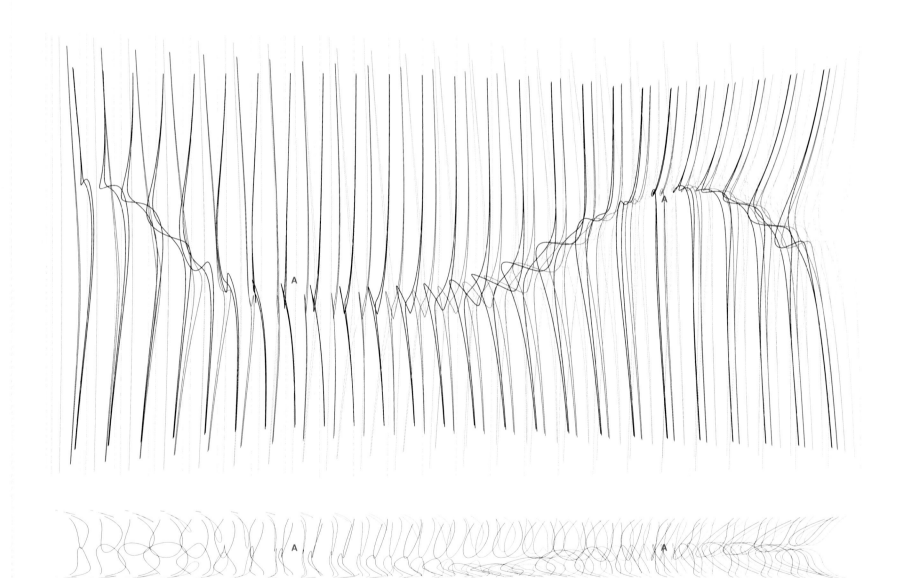

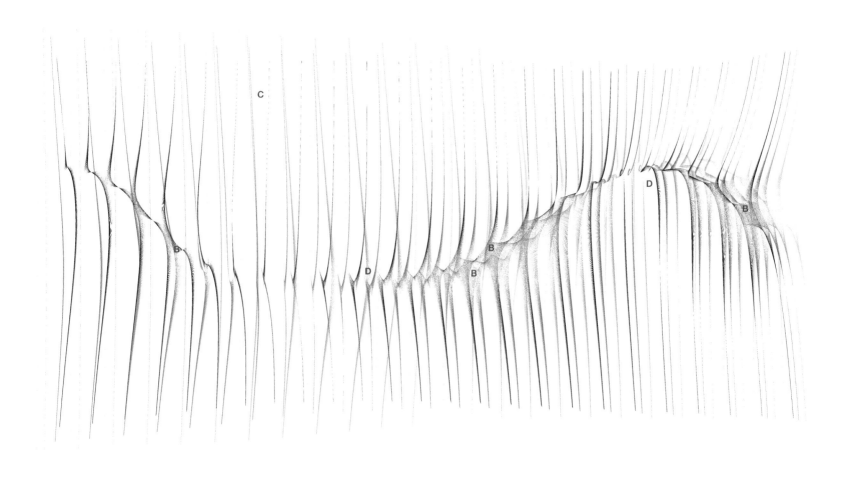

Dynamical System Development with Springs, Particle Fields, and Attached Surface Inflections

A   Least Range of Surface Inflection
B   Greatest Range of Surface Inflection

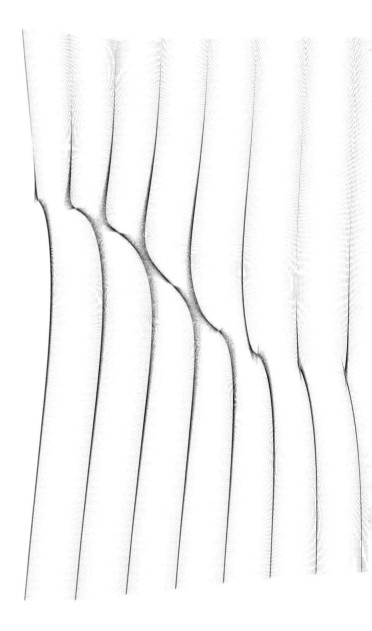

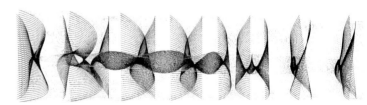

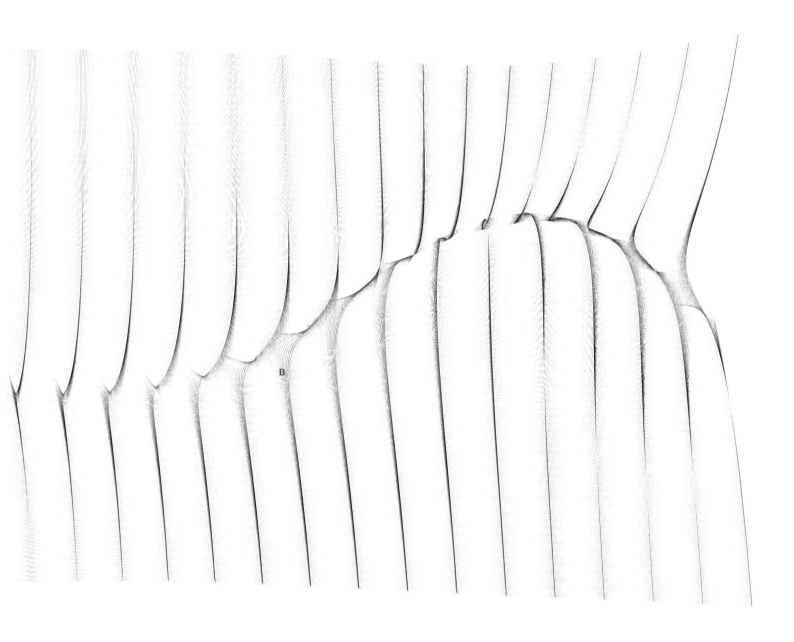

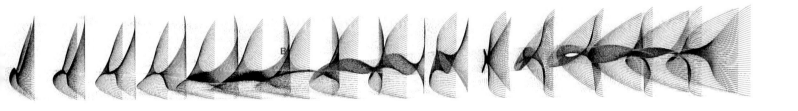

Sectional Model. Relationship between Roof and Inhabitable Surface

Site Model. Relationship between Roof and Landscape

Site Model

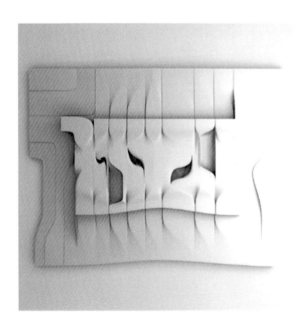

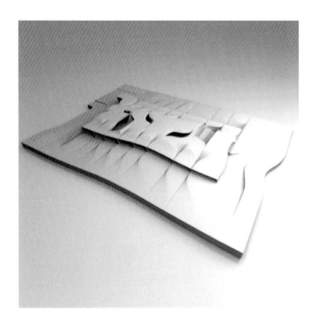

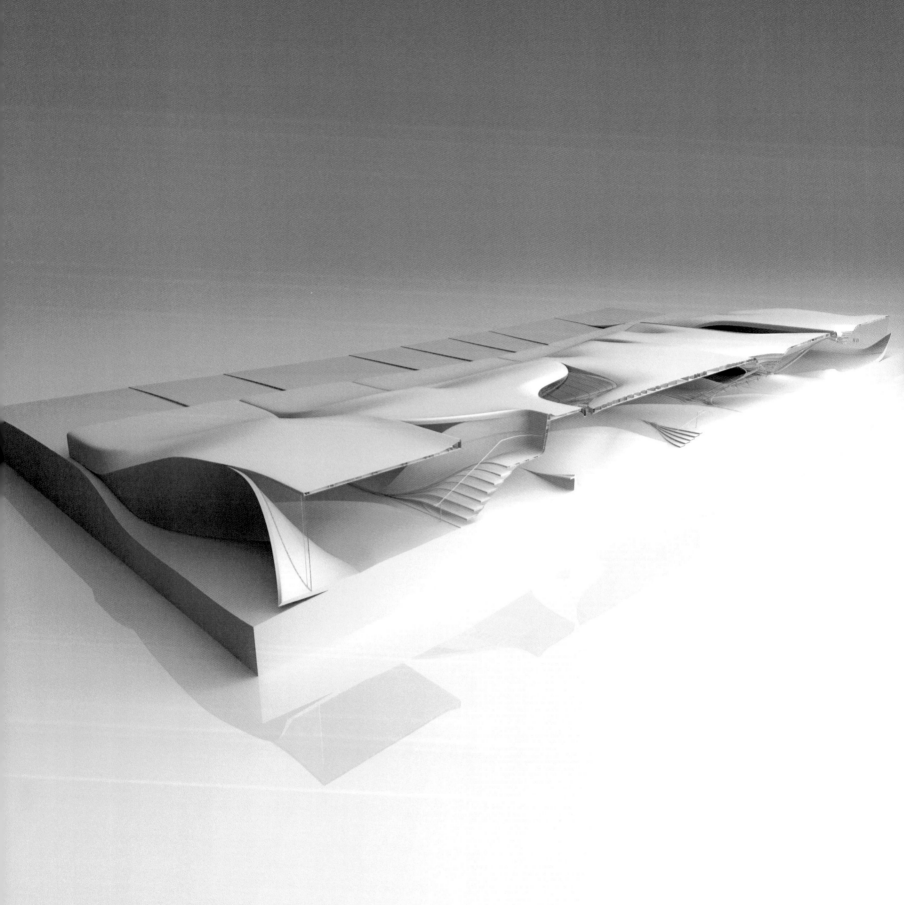

Site Plan. Continuity of Landscape Topography into Building Interior

A Bar
B Café
C Stairs

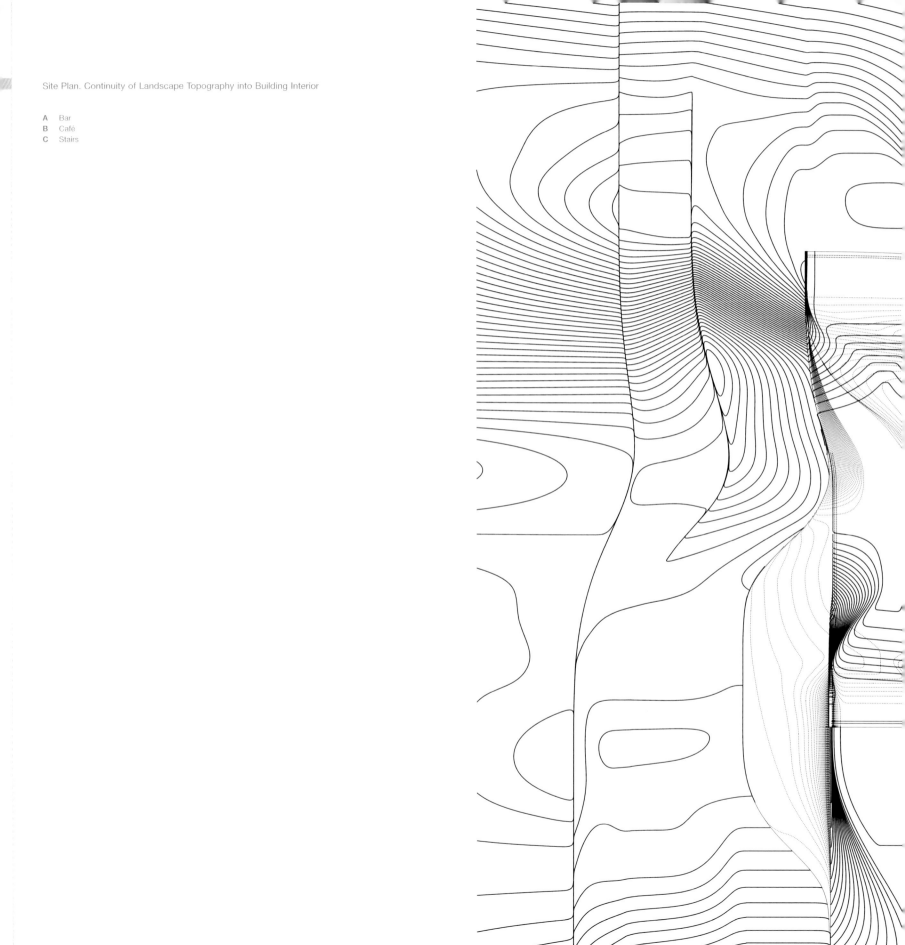

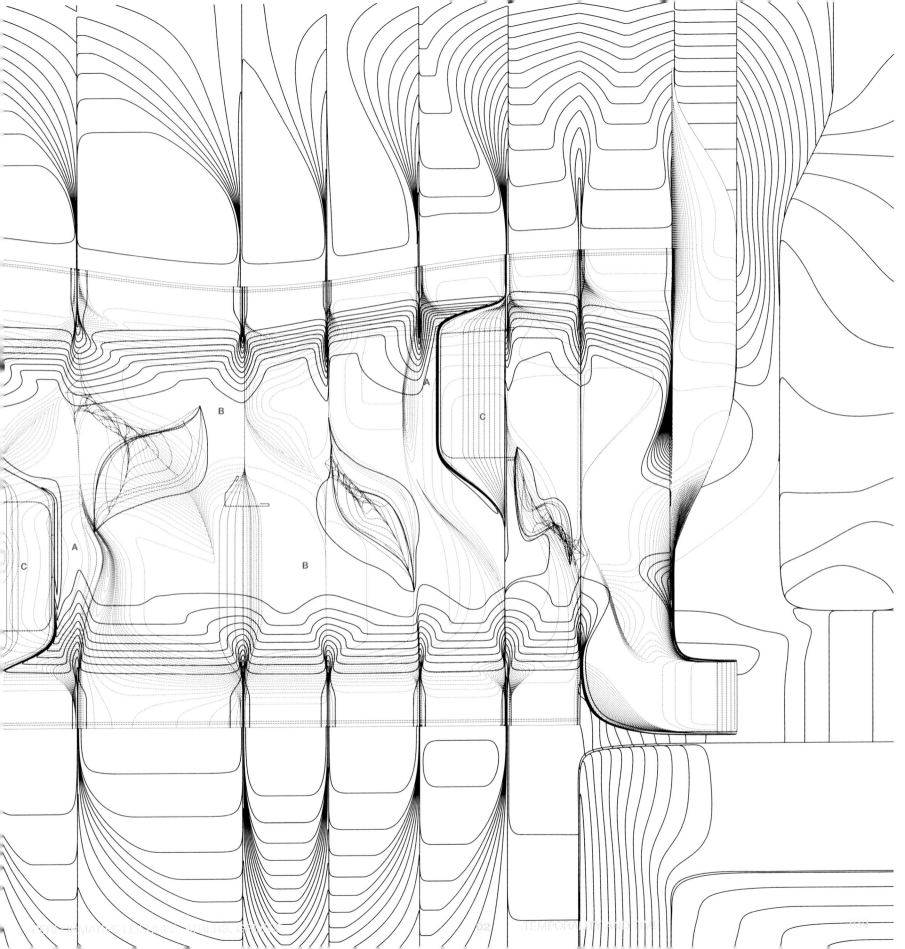

Building Elevation. Topographic Drawing of Building Surfaces

A   Top of Roof, +4 meters
B   Highest Point of Inhabitable Surface, +0.7meters
C   Ground Level, +0 meters
D   Lowest Point of Inhabitable Surface, -0.5 meters

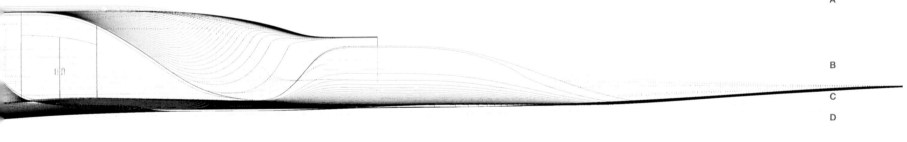

A

B

C

D

Interior View. Spaces for Hybridized Leisure Activities

Entry View

Detail View. Roof Aperture

Interior View. Landscape of Inflected Surfaces

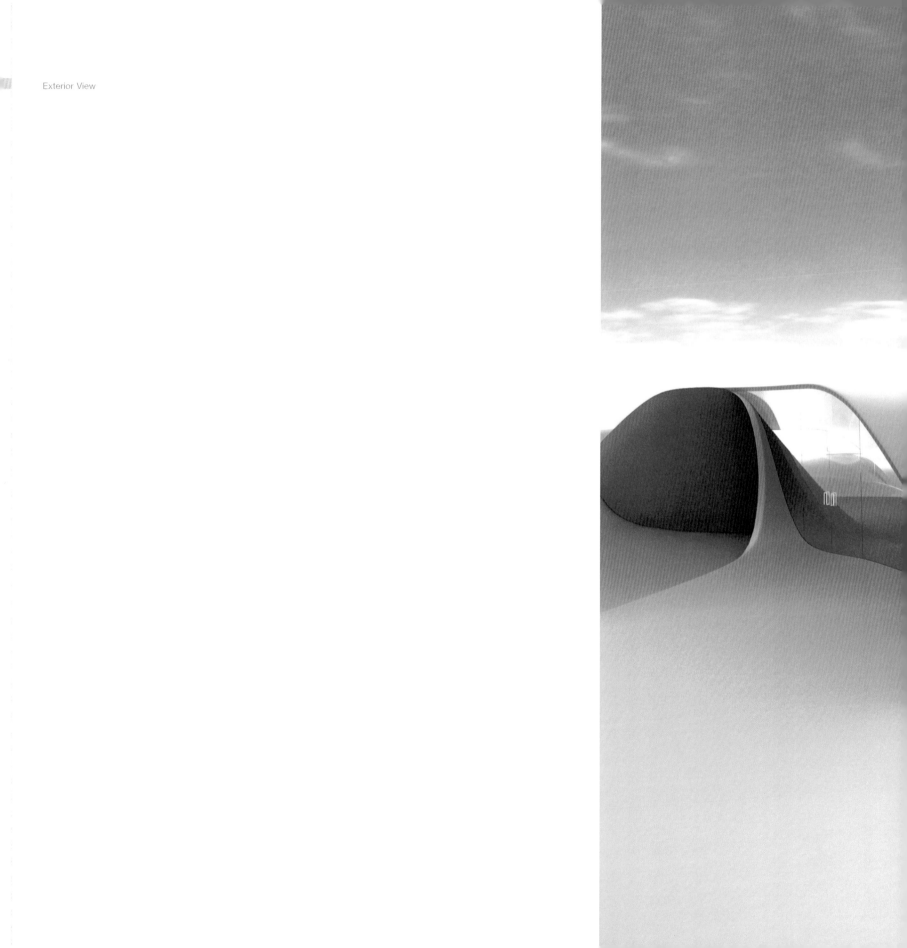

Interior View. Stairway/Seating and Sunbathing Area

PROJECT 02 INHABITING THE VECTOR

Reebok Flagship Store
Shanghai, China, 2004–

The flagship store for Reebok Asia is planned to be the first of a series of shops to be distributed through eastern China over the next ten years. The site of the flagship is in the Xintiandi district of Shanghai, a lively commercial area frequented by both locals and tourists. The challenge of the project was to develop a design that would accommodate the needs of a flagship store as well as allow both change over time and redeployment in other localities. Each satellite store had to be unique, responding to specific constraints such as the required inventory or local site conditions, while simultaneously communicating a common theme—Reebok's brand strategy, launched in 2003: "Wear the Vector: Outperform." The desire for simultaneous unity, variability, and adaptability necessitated thinking about the design through time and devising a system that could generate unforeseeable organizations.

These requirements led us to use a dynamical system technique that relied on a thermodynamic or open-ended model of temporality. Using the software Maya, the dynamical system was structured with multiple low-intensity pressures that corresponded to the allocation of merchandise throughout the store. Another higher-intensity pressure registered the constant influx of materials, merchandise, and people. The system also included a series of free pressures located around the perimeter of the store. The relationships among these forces were tested iteratively by varying the pressures' elasticity and mass. The aim was to inflect the lower-intensity pressures, or arrangement of merchandise, with the higher-intensity pressures corresponding to the movement of people and goods. In other words, the interior would be activated by a flow from the exterior: the store's users would literally inhabit a vector. The differences between the high and low pressures generated trajectories within the system. Once we refined the relationships to generate the desired trajectories, we added a particle field that reacted to differences in the system. The system was adjusted further until the particles produced a pattern that correlated to the potential movement of people through the store. The system of pressures and particles could then be altered and reprogrammed to meet the unique requirements of each store—from large urban outlets featuring many products to small suburban shops with only a small sampling of lines.

The system was then applied specifically to design the flagship store, which was intended to serve three main uses: a retail outlet, showroom for Reebok retailers to view and select merchandise, and venue for public relations events and product launches—such as appearances by Reebok's spokesperson Yao Ming. We used the dynamical system we had developed, parametrically adjusting the intensity of the pressures to the specific requirements of the store. For example, we shifted the pressures corresponding to the distribution of goods to accommodate the requirement for a shoe bar on the second floor, while the high-intensity pressure was increased to reflect the tremendous numbers of buyers and merchandise flowing into the store. The modulation of these constraints led to the emergence of linear groupings of varying densities within the particle field. The system was actualized[08] by connecting the particles with lines to generate curves and surfaces: the more particles or points regulating the curves, the more intense the transformations in the resulting surface. Lower densities of particles produced less intense transformations, such as textures on walking surfaces; medium-density accumulations gave rise to lines and surfaces that could be indented to create coves; and high densities of particles were connected with lines that could bifurcate to generate stairs.

In the lobby, for example, low-density accumulations produce textures on the floor and a vertical projection screen; medium-density lines are manipulated to form surfaces for shelving and seating as well as an interior skin that wraps around the store inside the existing building facade. The shoe bar also features several different densities of lines: medium-density lines generate areas for sitting and trying on shoes as well as lighting patterns in the ceiling; high-density lines give rise to bifurcations that create openings in walls and a staircase up to the third level. On the third level, low-density accumulations generate textured walking surfaces, medium-density lines become indentations in the ceiling for lighting, and high-density lines generate openings that afford views onto the shoe bar below.

A maximum number of affects[09] generated from the dynamical system are retained in the actualized formation, allowing uses to vary flexibly depending on the season and event. In the lobby, areas that normally serve as display or fitting areas can be converted to seating for marketing events. As one moves from the ground to the second level, patterns in the floor smoothly merge into surfaces for shelving, seating, or walking. The affects also are activated differently depending on the size and age of the user: children may climb on surfaces that adults use for sitting. The store manager can choreograph the space to an extent by determining the placement of products. The occupation of the space only emerges through users' negotiations with the space and merchandise.

Material and construction systems are selected that retain and even increase the formation's affects by giving rise to a range of climates and ambient conditions. The store is composed of a prefabricated semi-monocoque aluminum shell hung from the structure of an existing building. The interior skin of the store is made of clear vacuum-formed acrylic. The vacuum-forming process changes the molecular structure of the panels, generating affects in the movement of light over the surface. Similarly, most of the panelized surfaces not intended for circulation are made of laminated and molded fiberglass. In the molding process, the fiberglass develops affects that change depending on its use. Patterns indented into the fiberglass ceiling also help to produce diverse qualities of light.

The actualized formation does not conform to any previous model or type for a store. Instead, the form emerges from the relationships among the pressures of merchandise turnover, allocation, and user movements in the dynamical system. The system allows for the modification of inputs depending on local requirements and context. Thus, variability is accomplished through modification of the process rather than simply through shifts in scale or variation of parts. Changing the process rather than the components yields transformations in qualities and attributes—stretching, thickening, sharpening, or dulling, for example—that produce distinct affects, allowing interactivity with users to be maximized. The heightened variability and responsiveness made possible through dynamical system techniques will allow Reebok's stores to become singular urban attractors, with benefits for both the company and its consumers.

Dynamical Particle System for Xintiandi Site

A   High Density of Particles
B   Linear Groupings of Varying Densities of Particles
C   Low Density of Particles

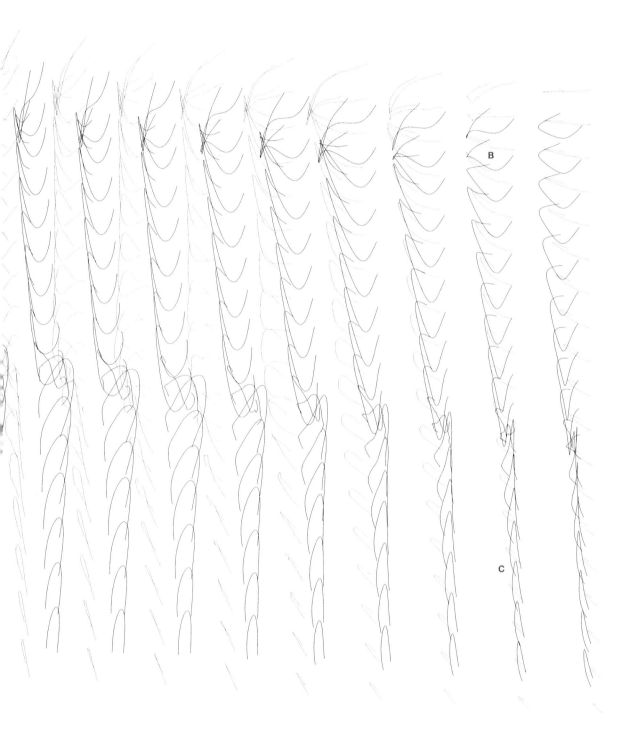

B

C

Adjusting Particle Density and Collisions Yielding Curves and Surfaces

A   Heavy Surface Modulation
B   Medium Surface Modulation
C   Light Surface Modulation
D   Trajectory 1
E   Trajectory 2

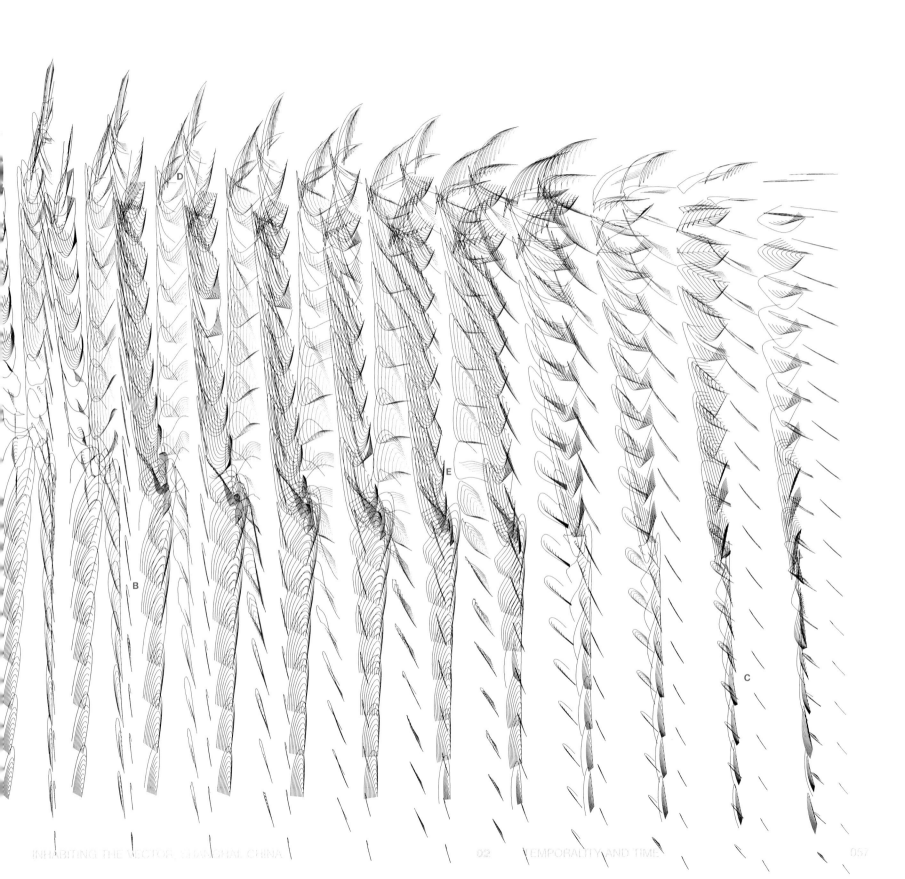

Model

Model

Sectional Model

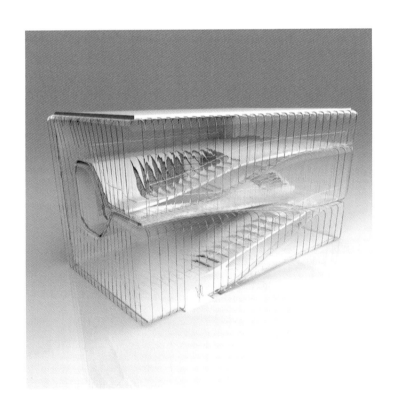 

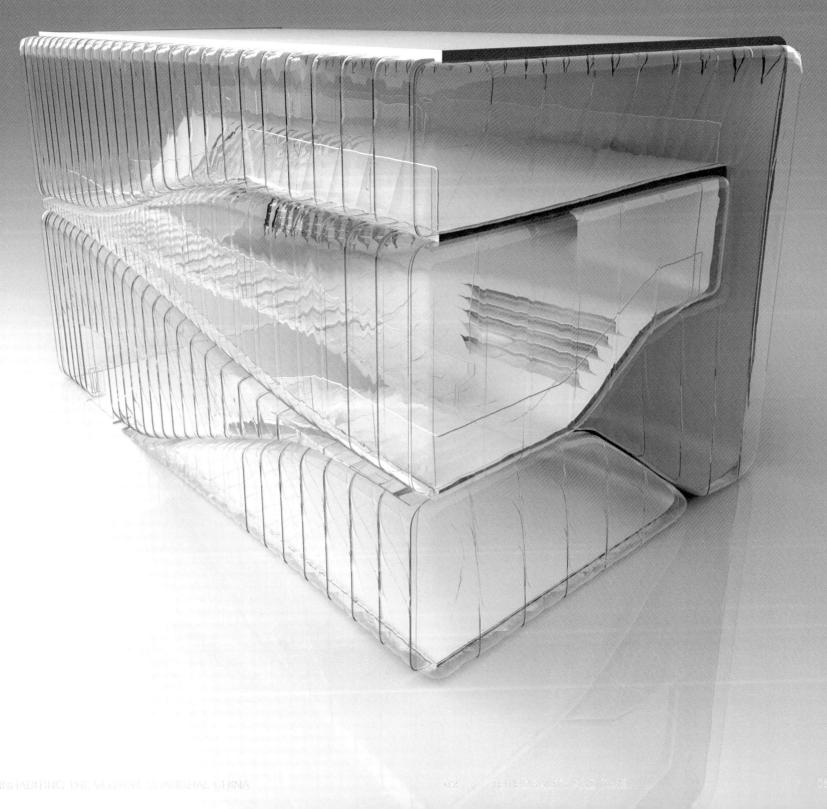

Second Level. Relationship of Second Floor to
Surface Modulation Pattern

First Level. Relationship of First Level Plan to
Surface Modulation Pattern

A   Display/Fitting or Seating for Marketing Events
B   Stairs to Second Level
C   Entry
D   Passage to Cross-Branded Space and D.J. Booth
E   Passage to Stockroom
F   Shoe Fitting Area
G   Shoe Bar
H   Seating/Shelving or Walking
I   Stairs to Third Level

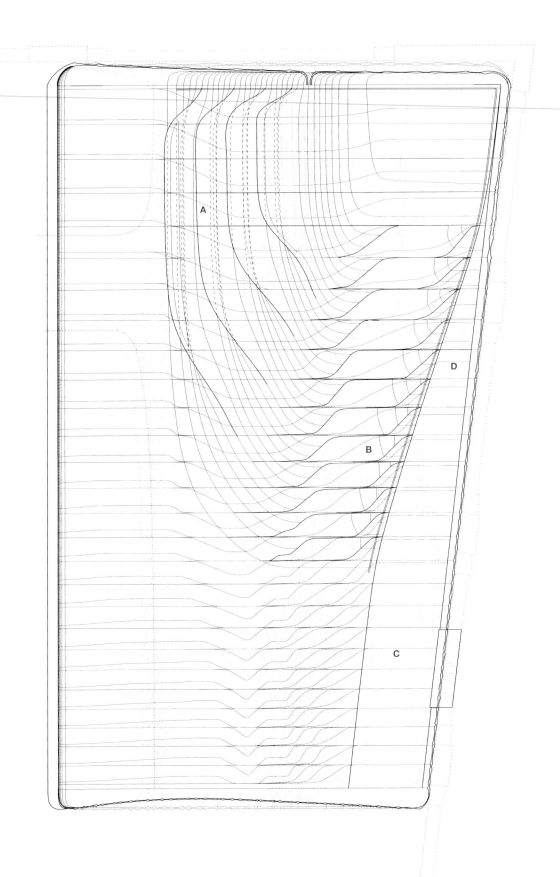

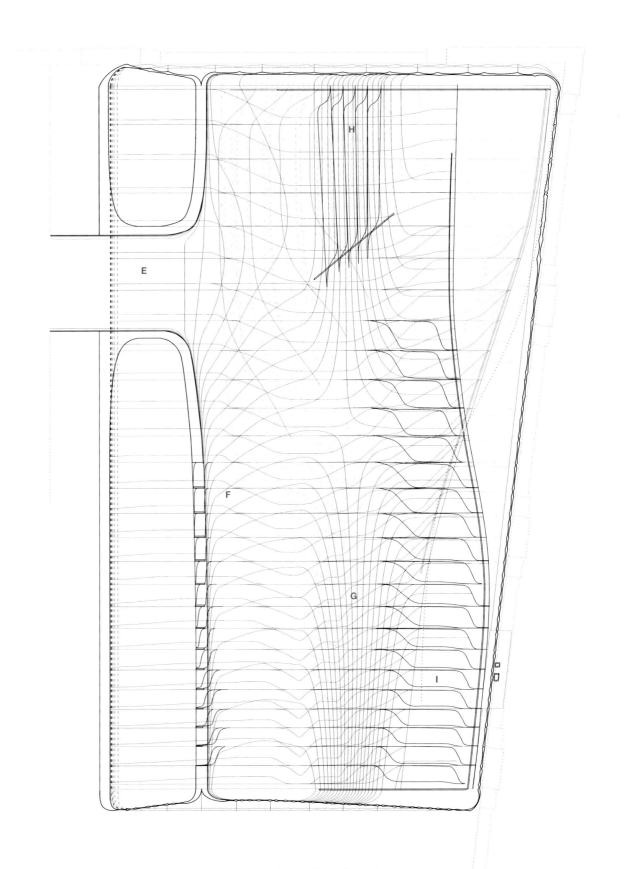

Elevation Formation. Interior
Glazing Pattern

A   Second Level, +6.3 meters
B   First Level, +2.7 meters
C   Entry Level, +0 meters

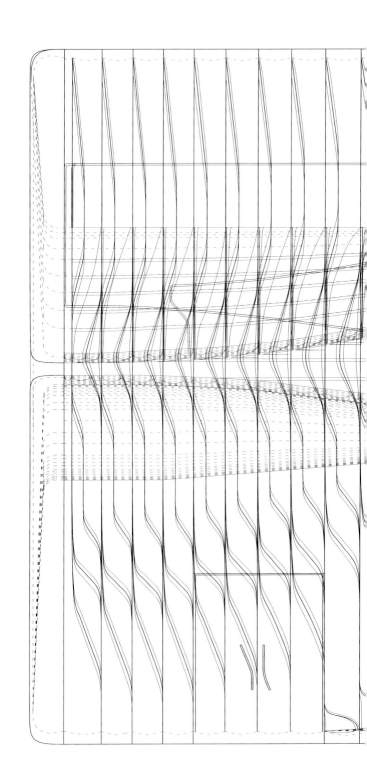

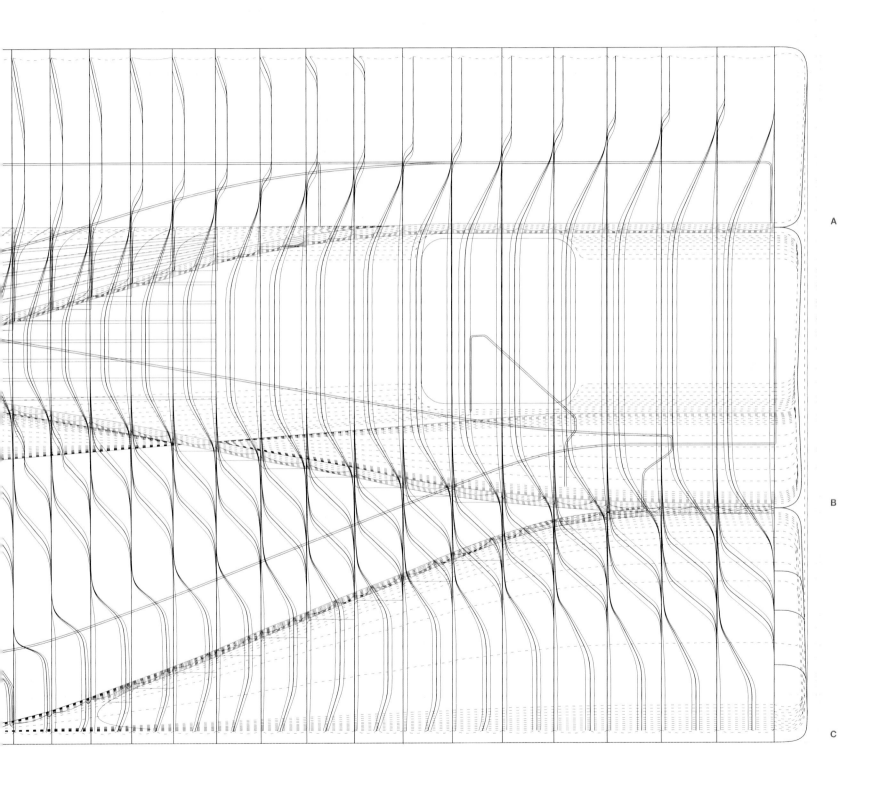

A

B

C

Interior View. Entry Level with Low, Medium and High Intensity Surface Modulation

View from Pedestrian Walkway in the Existing Building

Interior View. First and Second Floors

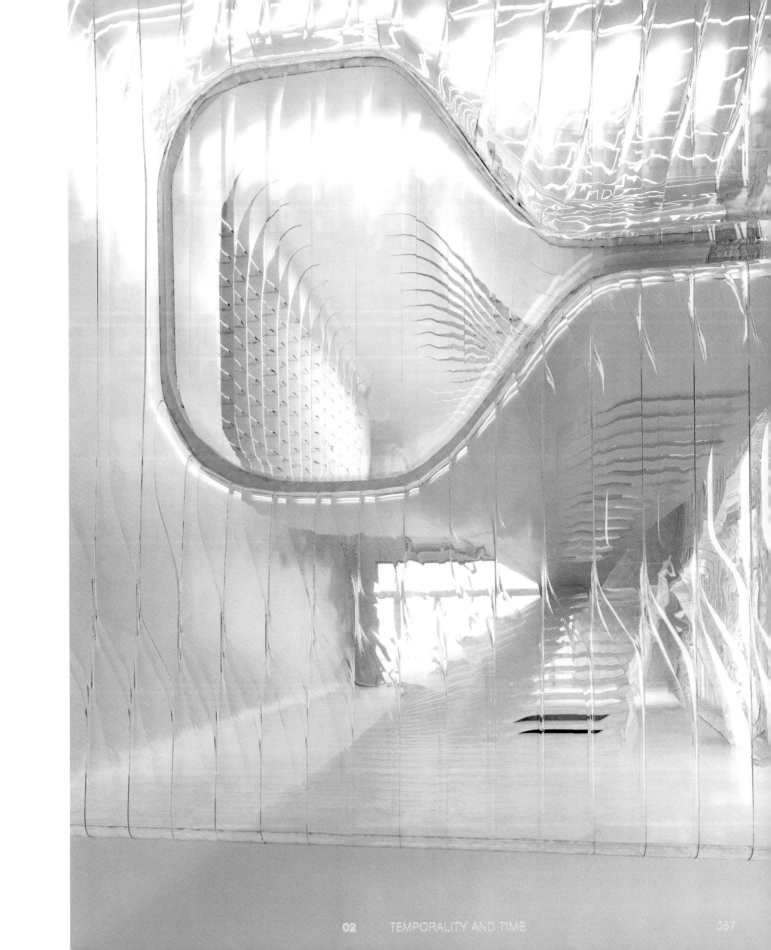

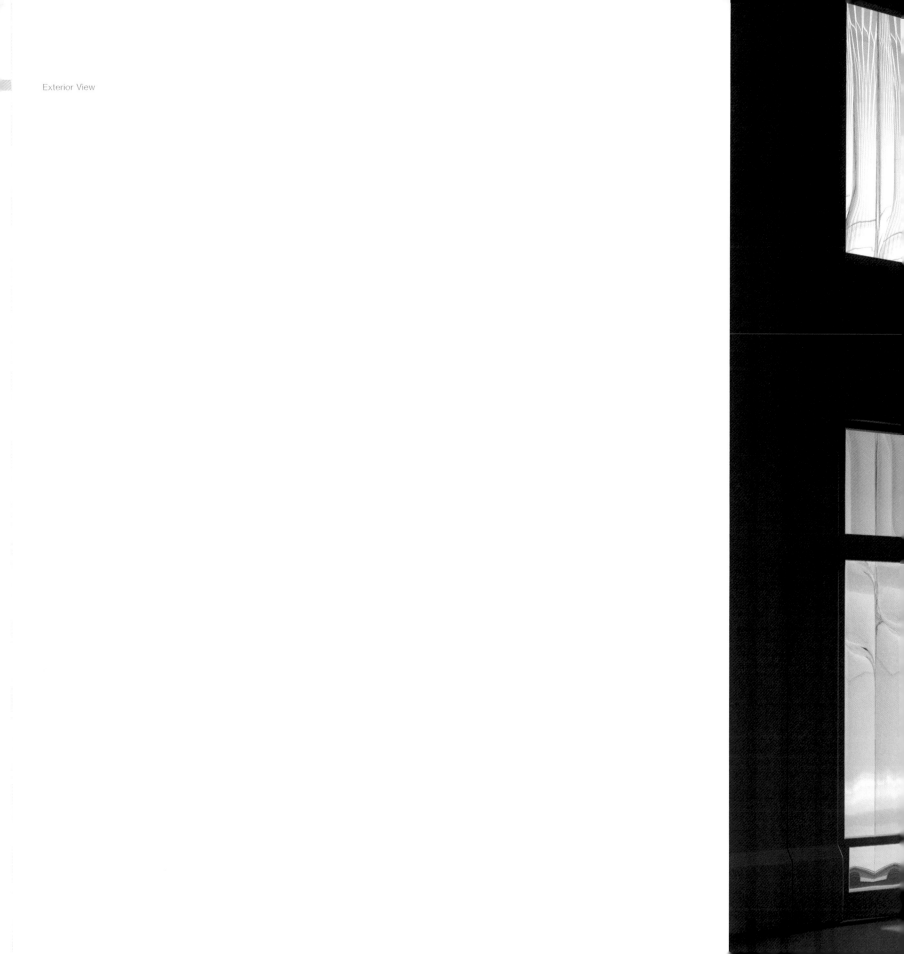

Interior View, Second Floor Shoe Bar

Interior View, Third Level, High [...] Modulation C[...]

01   Manuel DeLanda, *Intensive Science & Virtual Philosophy* (New York: Continuum, 2002), 82.

02   David L. Hull, *Science as a Process* (Chicago: University of Chicago Press, 1988), chapter 4.

03   DeLanda, 82–83.

04   Shape-shifting is not a technique exclusive to Alias/Wavefront. Equivalent operations can be performed, for instance, using metaclay objects in the software Softimage.

05   For discussion on actualization please refer to page 077.

06   For discussion on affects please refer to pages 136–137.

07   For discussion on affordances please refer to page 138.

08   For discussion on actualization please refer to page 077.

09   For discussion on affordances please refer to page 138.

03 VIRTUAL AND ACTUAL

To produce design innovation, technological practices use techniques that incorporate the *virtual*. By virtual, I do not mean virtual reality or simulations created in the computer, although the computer provides designers with an important tool to access the virtual. I am interested, rather, in the concept of the virtual that comes from mathematics and philosophy. Within these fields, the virtual comprises all that an object can be imagined to become. The virtual is a space of potentialities. Unlike the *actual*, which can be measured quantitatively and therefore exists in metric space, the virtual is nonmetric and contains qualities—or aspects that cannot be quantified. As I began to explain in Chapter 02, the virtual, this space of potentialities, is what allows temporal techniques to be generative—in other words, to give rise to formal, spatial, and material innovations.

In this chapter, I attempt to clarify the potential role of the virtual in the design process. To begin, I explain the difference between the relationship of the virtual to the actual and that of the possible to the real, as well as the implications of this distinction on the traditional architectural concepts of type and program. The process by which technological practices access the virtual through temporal techniques such as dynamical systems and transformational procedures is described in detail. Last, three projects are analyzed to illustrate how designers can actualize the virtual into works of architecture that propagate new spatial and cultural effects.

THE VIRTUAL AND THE ACTUAL VERSUS THE POSSIBLE AND THE REAL

Whereas conventional architecture firms typically operate in the realms of the possible and the real, technological practices think in terms of the virtual and the actual. What may at first seem to be merely a semantic distinction is in fact, quite important. The difference is that in the translation from the possible to the real, nothing emerges that was not already known, whereas the transition from the virtual to the actual always involves the emergence of something previously unanticipated. For example, an architect may look at two possibilities for the design of a house: one with two bedrooms and the other with three. By building one of these options in reality, no new effects or outcomes are generated, since there is a direct correspondence between possibility and reality. They both exist in the realm of the metric, or that which can be quantified. The virtual, on the other hand, is a space of potentialities that are unquantifiable and still unknown. The effects of the virtual may be actualized in metric space, becoming tangible, material, or knowable. Yet, the process of actualization always entails discovery because the virtual itself has no specific form; it is never the same as the actual.[01]

To make these terms clearer, we can look at the example of a campfire—an assemblage in which the relationship of virtual and actual changes constantly. As the direction and force of the wind change, so does the fire's shape, altering the distribution, pattern, and intensity of light and heat produced. These qualities of light and heat are *virtualities* because they contain the potential to give rise to a wide range of activities or effects, not all of which are known. As the fire changes, so does the potential for various activities around it. Humans negotiate the variable intensities of heat and light to determine the most suitable environments for tasks such as sleeping, cooking, and warming one's hands.[02] These various behaviors and arrangements are actualizations of the virtual. The relationship between the virtual and actual is not one-to-one; nor can it be reduced to simple cause and effect. Instead, the affiliation is marked by a degree of abstraction that enables it to be simultaneously operative, incomplete, and unpredictable.

VIRTUALITIES VERSUS TYPE AND PROGRAM

The example of the campfire illustrates another important difference between the dichotomies of virtual/actual and possible/real: whereas conventional practices tend to see a building's function as relatively static, technological practices aim to create works of architecture with changeable uses. I call these latter works *formations* rather than buildings to denote that they are still in the process of becoming. Even after they are actualized, formations contain virtualities—the potential to generate new uses and proliferating effects. In the example of the campfire, there is no fixed relationship between the form of the flames and their function. Instead, the uses of the fire shift constantly in response to its participants and to changing environmental conditions.

Formations thus mark a radical break from two key concepts of conventional architecture: type and program. Conventional architectural thinking relies on typology, a way of classifying buildings by their functions that dates to the eighteenth century. According to the proponents of typology, a building's program or essential function is directly tied to an idealized or original form. Type connotes that which allows the identity of a building—its use—to be read from its appearance.[03] Thus, the thinking goes, a house should look like a house and a prison should be legible as a prison. Building types are based on identity, analogy, and difference. Similarly, the functionalist concept of architectural program seeks to fix relationships between spaces and their uses. Conventional program diagrams represent a building's areas as boxes connected by lines of circulation. They reduce occupation and interaction within spaces to abstractions: spaces are reductively labeled as serving the functions of "living" or "dining." Missing from these diagrams, however, is the dynamism of users' movements and interactions in space.

Designing with the virtual abolishes fixed types and programs. Rather than housing a static, predetermined arrangement of functions within an established representational envelope, formations develop uses in response to their occupants and contexts. These uses are connected to the form directly rather than through representation. Formations possess this ability to catalyze new uses and responses because they retain an element of virtuality from their development.

THE VIRTUAL AND TEMPORAL TECHNIQUES

In Chapter 02, I describe the features of temporal techniques such as generative and transformational methods. All of these techniques incorporate elements of virtuality, enabling them to give rise to designs that continue to change even after they are actualized. To explain more clearly how technological practices work with the virtual, I would like to focus for a moment on two specific techniques: dynamical systems, a kind of generative technique, and transformational methods.

A dynamical system is a concept taken from mathematics: in such systems, a fixed rule describes the time dependence of a point in geometrical space. The swing of a clock pendulum or the flow of water in a pipe, are two examples of dynamical systems. The fixed rule, which often takes the form of a differential or difference equation, describes the state of the system at a short interval in the future. Given an initial position or point, it is possible to determine all future points by repeating the algorithm, each iteration advancing time a small step. The collection of the points yielded is known as a *trajectory*. Technological practices are interested in using dynamical systems for several reasons. First, dynamical systems model real-world material phenomena and properties and can capture the process of material formation. Thus, design processes based on dynamical systems are nonrepresentational; they do not rely on an intermediary model or analogical system outside of themselves. Working with dynamical systems allows a direct correspondence between a system, its materialization, and the actualized formation. Second, instead of moving from the possible to the real—that is, merely materializing that which is already known, dynamical systems allow designers to work through a process of development that is simultaneously design and research. Third, under certain conditions—namely, when they are pushed far from equilibrium—dynamical systems have the potential to yield new organizations and forms; hence, they contain virtuality.

The advent of the computer, and of software such as Maya in particular, has enabled the rapid calculation and modeling of dynamical systems—and has allowed technological practices to access their potential. Dynamical systems modeled in the computer comprise two types of conditions or parts. One type is quantitative, or numerically defined: it includes all those factors that the computer program allows the designer to control; for example, the parameters of the system's geometry or the

strength of relationships between parts. The interaction of these parametrically controlled components results in pressure fields and differences—akin to the differences between high and low pressure in weather systems—which result in energy flows or trajectories. The variations in the speeds of trajectories constitute the non-numerical or virtual part of a dynamical system because they can give rise to any number of possible outcomes. In the example of the storm, the difference in the speeds of wind currents generates a potential for some new form of organization—a tornado—to emerge. As the differences in speeds grows more extreme, the system moves farther from equilibrium and its potential to give rise to new organizations—in other words, virtuality—becomes maximized.

In using dynamical systems to generate formations, architects often begin by creating a field of pressures correlated to the project's real-world conditions: these might include the pressures exerted by neighboring roads on the site, circulation flows, building use, or structural loads. The gradients between these discrete pressures generate trajectories with varying rates of change. The differences between the rates of these trajectories contain the virtual—that is, the potential to generate a new pattern of organization. The pressure field is then applied to entities modeled in the computer, typically selected from methods provided by the software and bearing names such as IK chains, meta-objects, or springs. These entities behave in the same way as trees put into motion by a tornado, to return to the example used earlier. The designer chooses an entity or method that corresponds with the aims of the project. All the methods have specific properties that can be parametrically controlled by the architect—including geometry, quantity, method of connection (for example, with a pin or rotation joint), potential zones of influence, elasticity, and rigidity. Just as the mass, size, and shape of the trees influence how they interact with the tornado, entities in the dynamical system produce their own resistances and pressures, which affect the system as a whole. By adjusting the parameters of the properties and relationships between the pressure field and modeling entities, the designer directs and shapes the dynamical system.

It is important to note that the entities in the system do not take the form of the trajectories but, instead, respond to the rates of

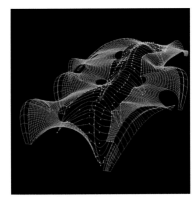

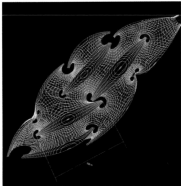

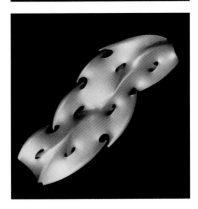

Chavasse Park, Liverpool, UK. Philip Johnson with Cecil Balmond, 2002

Computer Model showing Ridges and Valleys of Chavasse Park, Liverpool, UK. Philip Johnson with Cecil Balmond, 2002

Final Form. Chavasse Park, Liverpool, UK. Philip Johnson with Cecil Balmond, 2002

change between multiple trajectories. This means that there is no direct cause and effect (in other words, one applies a pressure and the entity bends). Instead, multiple pressures interact in unpredictable ways to generate spontaneous trajectories, patterns, and results. If the constituent pressure gradients create enough difference in the system, virtualities are generated and the system may become emergent.[04] Emergence is the spontaneous occurrence of an organization or a behavior that is greater than the sum of its parts. The emergence is a change in kind; it is unknown and resembles nothing that we can already see. The example used above, the tornado, is an emergent phenomenon— a new organization that is not a version of the winds that precede it. As in all dynamical systems, the probability of emergence is increased when the system is far from equilibrium— for example, in the presence of extreme pressure differences in the atmosphere. Systems that exhibit emergent behavior become a source of differentiation and destabilize the existing state.[05]

Architects working with dynamical systems aim to establish conditions that will generate emergence. Emergence does not occur automatically. To the contrary, the architect must precisely calibrate the differences and relationships between pressures and techniques. This often requires making repeated adjustments and testing the technique iteratively. How does the designer know when a system has emerged? Since it is conceivable that a dynamic system may yield several emergent states, the designer must apply his or her intelligence to evaluate when a new organization has surfaced, and whether this state fulfills the aims of the project. Thus, working with dynamical systems does not abolish analytical thinking. Instead, bottom-up processes must always be used in tandem with the designer's critical faculties.

Once the architect determines that a dynamical system has reached an emergent state and has achieved the aims of the project, the system is transferred to metric space and becomes an actualized formation. Actualization does not mean that the system is constructed but, rather, that it becomes concretized as something with quantitatively measurable features. A system can be actualized but remain unbuilt, existing only in three-dimensional models. The actual does not resemble the form of the virtual since, by nature, the structure of the virtual cannot be frozen. However, the actualized formation bears traces of the virtualities, transformations, and other critical factors that contributed to its development.

Like dynamical systems, transformational techniques also allow technological practices to access the virtual. Transformational methods entail the manipulation of continuous surfaces or objects through procedures such as cutting, folding, and stretching. The objects are structured as sets of interconnected points in such a way that operating on one area of the object induces changes to all other areas. The precise manner in which an individual change will be redistributed over the whole cannot be predicted. Each transformational procedure applies a pressure on the surface that generates other transformations across the surface. The interactions between these transformations comprise the technique's virtual element. For example, an architect interested in using transformational techniques might operate on a NURB (non-rationalized Bezier) curve, an object structured by a series of interconnected curves. Shifting one curve in the NURB surface results in changes in nearby curves, which modify all the other curves, thereby altering the overall form of the object. The greater the differences between the transformations, the greater the virtuality contained within the object. Similar to working with a dynamical system, the designer develops the transformational technique iteratively, adjusting the parameters of the object and the transformation until virtuality is maximized and the desired outcomes are achieved. Only then is the project actualized.

Transformational techniques, like dynamical systems, are non-representational. Objects modeled in the computer have material properties and are actualized directly; they do not stand for or represent anything else. Most importantly, the results of both types of technique cannot be predicted in advance; this constitutes their virtual element. Where dynamical systems and transformational techniques differ is the source of their virtuality: in dynamical systems, the virtual arises from the differences between rates of change in the trajectories; these differences then inflect an object or set of objects. In contrast, transformational techniques operate directly on an object, and virtuality develops in the differences between the resulting series of transformations. In both techniques, additional manipulations can be used to further refine the design at a more detailed scale.

VIRTUALITY AND FORMATIONS

Since they incorporate virtuality as part of their processes, temporal techniques such as dynamical systems and transformational methods allow designers to generate formations that share several key characteristics: First, as I mentioned earlier, formations retain an element of virtuality from their developmental processes, which gives them the potential to generate unexpected effects. These virtualities often manifest themselves in formal features that afford numerous potential uses. Second,

formations assemble multiple parts within a single entity without canceling out the differences between constituent elements.[06] Differentiation is not accomplished through variety—that is, by collecting myriad independent members each suited for a particular purpose—or through extension—by simply augmenting the number or size of spaces. Instead, formations absorb many elements in a way that is irreducible: they cannot be divided without changing their qualities. Third, formations do not remain static but develop continuously through feedback with their users and contexts, leading to the possibility of larger-scale cultural effects. The meaning of these attributes will become clearer in the examples below. All three cases illustrate the process of actualizing the virtual into a catalytic formation.

IRREDUCIBLE FORMATION: CHAVASSE PARK

For an example of a project generated using dynamical systems, we can look at the Chavasse Park shopping center in Liverpool, England, designed by Philip Johnson in collaboration with Cecil Balmond and the engineering firm Arup (2002). The project presented several challenges: it was hoped that the new center's retail and entertainment facilities would revitalize the city center, provide an urban link to the old docks, and present an extraordinary large-scale spatial experience at the heart of the city. Balmond began by modeling a dynamical system in the computer, and inputting pressures correlated to various site conditions. The process was repeated iteratively until the virtualities within the system were maximized and an emergent state was generated, yielding a trajectory that Balmond called the "generative line."

At this point, a modeling method was selected with an eye toward achieving the center's goal of maximizing public use, openness, and spatial effects within a continuously varied two-story structure. Balmond selected a surface mesh, a technique that allows the integration of envelope, structure, and apertures in one continuous surface. After being placed into the environment of the dynamical model, the surface mesh responded to the differences in the rates of flow within the pressure field. Balmond iteratively adjusted the pressure differences in the system until the trajectory and mesh developed feedback, and an organization emerged that was distinct from both the form of the trajectory and that of the mesh. More adjustments were made to ensure that the final

Ice Storm, MAK, Vienna, Austria. Zaha Hadid with Patrik Schumacher, 2003
Ice Storm, MAK, Vienna, Austria. Zaha Hadid with Patrik Schumacher, 2003

formation met the objectives of the project. Once this occurred, the project was actualized in metric space.

As illustrated in this example, actualization occurs through an iterative process in which the designer aims to establish critical conditions between the pressure field and the modeling entity. In the final iteration of Chavasse Park, the formation separates from the virtual in time, but it retains its virtualities in metric space. The actualized formation reveals numerous qualities at a range of scales. Characteristics of tautness and looseness are evident in areas where the steel structure becomes denser or looser to expose more or less glass. The overall form is composed of many irreducible, seamlessly integrated parts: tension valleys where the surface lowers to meet the ground and compression ridges where it rises to form a roof. The form of the project continually varies in space, creating a series of dramatic interchanges between inside and outside. The final structure cannot be recognized immediately as a shopping center: it is not a representation of a static, idealized type. Part building and part landscape, the formation can be entered like an edifice but its contours prevent the user from taking any direct path. It must be discovered and negotiated as a terrain, challenging visitors to explore different ways of utilizing its spaces. Effects proliferate both at the scale of the individual user and at the larger scale of the city, as the shopping center forges new connections between urban residents and previously under utilized parts of the city.

UNEXPECTED EFFECTS: *ICE STORM*

As I suggested earlier, designing through virtuality challenges conventional notions of architectural type and program. *Ice Storm* (2003), an installation designed by Zaha Hadid and Patrik Schumacher for MAK, the Museum of Contemporary Art in Vienna, illustrates how formations destabilize established categories of use. To create the installation, the designers began by generating a dynamical system in the computer structured by three pressures or constraints: limitations on the space of the installation, the number of visitors in the gallery, and the paths of entry and exit in the exhibition space. Through an iterative process, Hadid and Schumacher maximized the differences in the pressures, generating trajectories. They then selected a modeling method appropriate to the goal of the exhibit, which was to provide an inhabitable environment that would highlight the interactivity between the human body and the installation itself by facilitating a variety of uses. Several meta-objects were placed at the perimeter of the exhibition space and exposed to the pressure gradients in the dynamical model. Under the influence of the pressure field and each other, the meta-objects were stretched and transformed until they spontaneously exhibited behaviors reciprocal to the pressure differences in the system. The meta-objects dynamically fused with each other to form a heterogeneous yet unified assemblage. This collective object resembled pieces of furniture that had melded into one other. In some cases, differences between meta-objects were negated, while in other places, individual objects retained their identities. The resulting formation cannot be categorized as furniture or space but, instead, is something in between. Its geometry cannot be reduced or divided without changing its virtualities.

To create *Ice Storm*, Hadid and Schumacher employed a process of design research and experimentation rather than following established rules of architectural program. The use of a dynamical system, with its embedded virtualities, as part of the design process results in variability—the ability of the formation to facilitate unexpected effects and multiple evolving uses. Catalytic formations give rise to geometries that avoid prescribed definition and that can be used and negotiated in multiple ways. Within *Ice Storm*, the virtualities that have been actualized into a formation continue to influence their users and environments as capacities of interaction, or *affordances*—a subject that is described in greater detail in Chapter 04. These capacities of interaction persist in the form of the project's heterogeneous surfaces—smooth, rough, hard, soft, convex, and concave—that results from the pressures of the virtual. These capacities support any manner of inhabitation. The formation's uses are not intrinsic; rather, they are triggered through repeated interaction with visitors. Leaning or walking on the formation activates a set of virtualities that are dormant when the surface is not in use. A virtual relationship that has been actualized can still change; the actual is only a momentarily tangible dimension of the virtual. The inventive living and lounging environments of *Ice Storm* thus promise new and continually evolving postures and modes of inhabitation.

FEEDBACK WITH USERS AND CONTEXTS: *MARSYAS*

The two previous examples focused on techniques that use the virtuality contained in dynamical systems. However, the virtual can also be engaged through transformational techniques. An example of this working method is illustrated by *Marsyas* (2002), an installation created by Anish Kapoor and Cecil Balmond for the Tate Modern Museum in London. To design the installation, Balmond and engineers at Arup began by writing a software program that would develop an initial idea or transformation iteratively into a series of dynamically variable models. Using this software, several transformational pressures, including gravity, a material resistance to gravity, and lateral forces, were applied to solid object models. The interaction between these pressures shaped the solid form, stretching and expanding it in ways that could not be predicted. These formal transformations were then studied, and material, form, and structure were developed iteratively and in tandem. The design was refined through successive cycles of feedback until the form and transformational pressures became correlated. When the designers were satisfied that the emergent relationship between transformation and form met their aims, the project was actualized in metric space.

Once constructed and installed in the space of the main hall at the Tate Modern, the final formation retained differences and virtualities from its development. Seams in the installation bore evidence of the project's transformation through stretching. Remarkably, the fabric and structure were executed in such a way that the formation exhibited no wrinkles in its form. Monolithic and continuous in shape, the formation nevertheless produced multiple spatial conditions that varied as the user moved under and around it, generating a complex play of perceptions. Context also played a crucial role: the placement of the formation within the rectangular volume of the Tate's main hall generated its own field of tensions and pressures. The installation was attached to the floor of the exhibition space at two ends. In the center, it opened and hovered above the mezzanine, allowing visitors a glimpse into its structure. From some angles, *Marsyas* appeared to be pushing the interior envelope of the gallery; from other perspectives, the room seemed to pressure the installation. If the formation had been placed in an open field, it would have generated entirely different visual and spatial experiences. Rather than being preconceived by the artists, the form of *Marsyas* was developed through an emergent process. The final formation resisted classical geometrical classification or definition.

VIRTUALITIES AND CATALYTIC FORMATIONS

Virtualities, once actualized into formations, propagate new virtualities and potentials. The virtual can never be known fully; at best, designers may elaborate on its qualities or describe its consequences.[07] The potential uses and implications of a formation such as Chavasse Park, *Ice Storm*, or *Marsyas* might yet be developed. Design innovations often require that new cultural uses be invented in order to activate latent virtualities. Formations are never static but, instead, are always open to further change; they continually catalyze new effects in users.[08]

Formations thus challenge traditional notions of architectural type and program, which are based on representational abstraction and reduction. In formations, uses are not designated in advance but instead, emerge through a dynamic process of feedback between the project's physical shape, its users, and its context. Catalytic formations suggest that the traditional notion of program be replaced with a concept of usefulness. Usefulness is an emergent condition, meaning that virtual and hitherto unknown ways of utilizing a formation may still evolve. Unlike program, usefulness does not designate a specific function or mode of occupation for a given space; instead, the aim is to generate conditions that allow different functions to be actualized with each instance of inhabitation. Hence program gives way to potential— the potential for interaction and change. In a catalytic formation, each individual uses the project's surfaces as they wish. Because the surface is differentiated, each participant, by interacting with the surface, influences the participant next to him or her and so on—with effects that cascade onto the whole. The formation thus constitutes an unfolding field of social interactions facilitated by its geometric articulation—in other words, it becomes catalytic.

The challenge for designers working with the virtual and actual is to produce architectural formations that can function as catalysts through their production and use. Actualized formations retain some of the virtualities developed in the process of their actualization. They continue to generate new effects and uses. Hence, feedback between the virtual and the actual is a vital component of the techniques used by technological practices.

Marsyas, Tate Modern, London, UK. Anish Kapoor with Cecil Balmond, 2002

Marsyas, Opening on Mezzanine Level at the Tate Modern, London, UK. Anish Kapoor with Cecil Balmond, 2002

PROJECT 03 VARIATIONS

Residence for a Fashion Designer
London, UK, 2002

The 6,000-square-foot weekend residence sits on a long, narrow, 120-acre site in the suburbs of London. The plot overlooks hills to the northwest and is bounded on its long sides by other houses. The client, a fashion designer, wanted a place that could serve both as a retreat and as a site to host seasonal runway events for friends and exclusive clients. It was decided to make the landscape, which featured irrigation wells and water retention ponds, an integral part of the house design. Each of these uses and components had an implicit temporality: the house had to be convertible for temporary uses for as little as four hours, while the landscape elements varied seasonally. To negotiate this complex range of uses and temporalities and to maximize the possibilities for integrating them in new ways, we used temporal techniques— specifically a dynamical system model that allowed us to create a continuous interchange between building and landscape.

The dynamical system was generated in the computer using the software Maya. Pressures were located at pivotal points on the site: at existing wells, in the direction of the views, and next to adjacent residences. In addition, an oscillating pressure was placed at the site of the house itself. Each of these pressures had a different rate of pulsation that corresponded to its temporality: the site, for example, consisted of pressures that varied seasonally while the pressures correlated to the house changed hourly and daily. By testing and modulating the strength, location, and oscillation rates of the pressures, we were able to generate enough pressure differences that trajectories formed within the system. Adjusting any single parameter shifted the form of the trajectories. In other words, the flow of pressure in the system generated affects that modified the system, creating a feedback loop. This pressure system was then applied to inverse-kinematic (IK) chains—geometries in Maya that are akin to skeletal systems with bones, joints, and specified degrees of rotation. The IK chains were distributed on the site in a regular grid pattern. After further modulations and adjustments of both the IK chains and the pressure system, a new pattern of organization spontaneously emerged. The IK chains aligned themselves within the general area of the residence and oscillated at different rates of change. The system was then actualized[09] by generating splines based on the movements of the IK chains. Slow rates of change in the IK chains were actualized as soft, planted landscape surfaces, while medium and fast rates of change became irrigation channels made of concrete and clad in fiberglass. Three differentiated channels were generated, with affordances that change depending on the season. For example, during the rainy season, the channels modulate drainage and irrigation, but can be converted to catwalks for fashion shows or to other uses such as sitting, sunbathing, and walking, during the dry months. A pool used as a retention pond in the wintertime can be used as a swimming hole in the summer months. These shifting affordances[10] form a gradient of uses.

The same technique of linking IK chains into curves and channels is applied to the house itself, so that landscape and building are smoothly linked. The residence is an intensification of the landscape: it contains more variation in a smaller area. Differences in the IK chains' rates of change in the dynamical system generate a range of surfaces in the residence and the envelope: IK chains with medium rates of change become inflections in the envelope and interior surfaces while IK chains with higher rates of change form openings in the building. On the south side of the house, the surface of the landscape folds to become the envelope of the building, generating affordances: the fold creates a private area where visitors can gather or play prior to entering the residence. Entering the hybridized building-and-landscape formation, users can choose to pass through towards the exterior channels in the north or to ascend a staircase to the second floor or the roof. The landscape and building are continuous: the landscape literally crosses the glass threshold of the house and enters the project, merging seamlessly with the surfaces of the house. Inside the residence, there are no clear thresholds between spaces; instead, walls and floors are continuous, maximizing the formation's affect and affordances.

For example, the house's surfaces afford numerous scales and speeds of circulation: the primary and slowest path comprises a continuous surface connecting all of the main spaces of the house, from the main entertainment area on the ground floor to the kitchen, multi-use space, and more private sleeping and bathing spaces on the upper level. This surface contains many affordances: on the ground floor, it provides a surface for walking and sitting; as it rises to the second level, it can be leaned or stepped upon. In the multi-use space, a sharply folded inflection within a slightly inclined surface allows groups to gather, while a gentle fold permits easy dispersal and spatial continuity. A second medium-speed path moves users from the ground to the second level and roof via a staircase. At the ground level, this surface provides affordances for leaning and sitting; the stairs themselves allow for walking or sitting. On the second floor, the surface affords the possibility for viewing or can function as a runway for fashion shows. The third and fastest path gives users access from the second level multi-functional space directly to the exterior landscape. The surface inflections that constitute the third form of circulation are more contained and afford

uses such as sitting and walking. The combination of these speeds of circulation and interstitial surfaces allows users a range of possible occupations that shift depending on the user. As particular affordances are activated they affect other users. For example, if one person leans against a surface on the ground floor, his or her action may inspire other guests to gather nearby; a crowd may eventually form and spill out into the landscape. If someone activates the same inflection by sitting on it, another series of affects follows that may lead to dispersal rather than gathering.

The structure and materiality of the formation are carefully selected and modulated to maximize its affects.[11] The house is made of a prefabricated concrete and aluminum semi-monocoque shell sheathed with fiberglass on the exterior and linoleum on the interior. The north side is clad in glass in order to maximize the view of the hills while forming a barrier between the environment and the residence. On the south side, surface openings are designed to maximize the range of light conditions that occur during different times of the day and year. The possibility of variation between light and dark, smooth and rough, and loud and quiet ambiences is intensified. Depending on the position of the viewer, the affects generated by a single surface can vary from opaque to translucent to transparent.

The actualized formation contains affordances that activate the virtual potentials developed during the design process. The affordances vary with use and context rather than being fixed and specified. The formation allows the everyday functions of living and more extraordinary events such as fashion shows to occur seamlessly and easily. The dynamic spatial relationships inside the residence and the continuity between building and landscape afford the potential for different users to activate and invent new patterns of occupation. Through use, the building and landscape may generate catalytic effects.

Dynamical System. Inverse Kinematics with NURBS Curves

A   Existing Well
B   Site of House Determined by Zoning

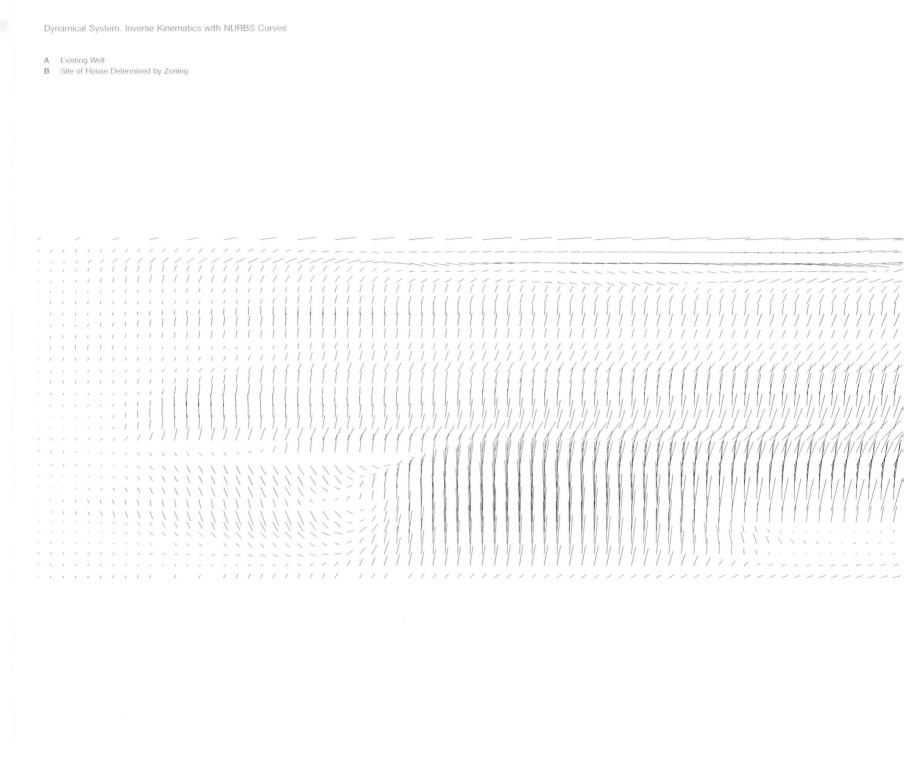

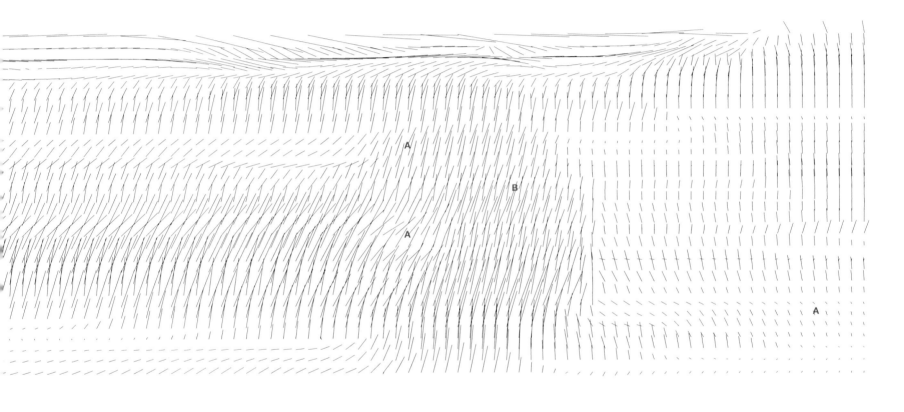

Dynamical System Incorporating Programmatic Uses

A   Slow Rate of Change
B   Medium Rate of Change
C   Fast Rate of Change

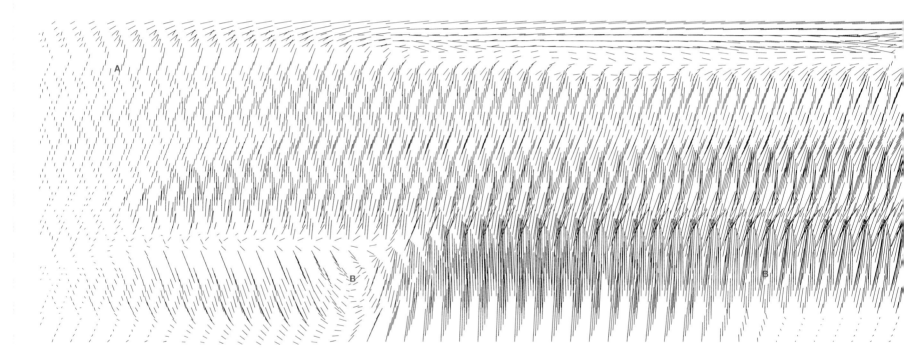

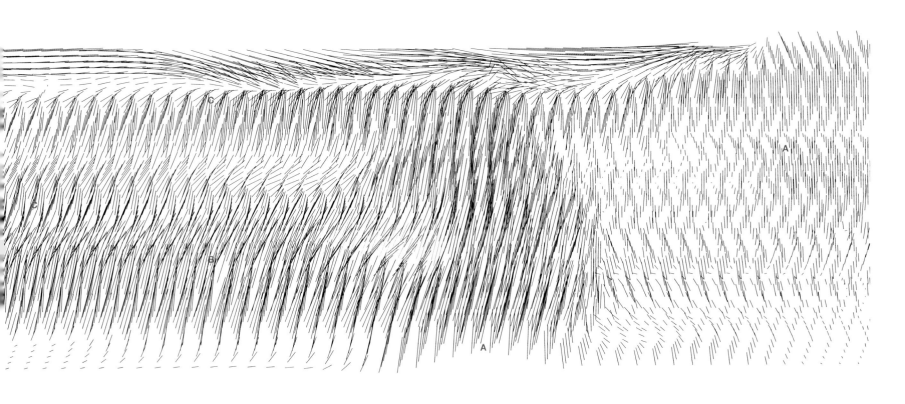

Site Model

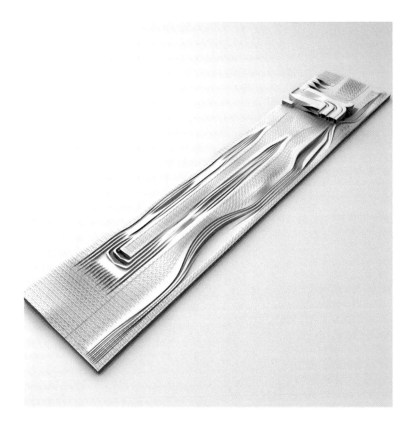

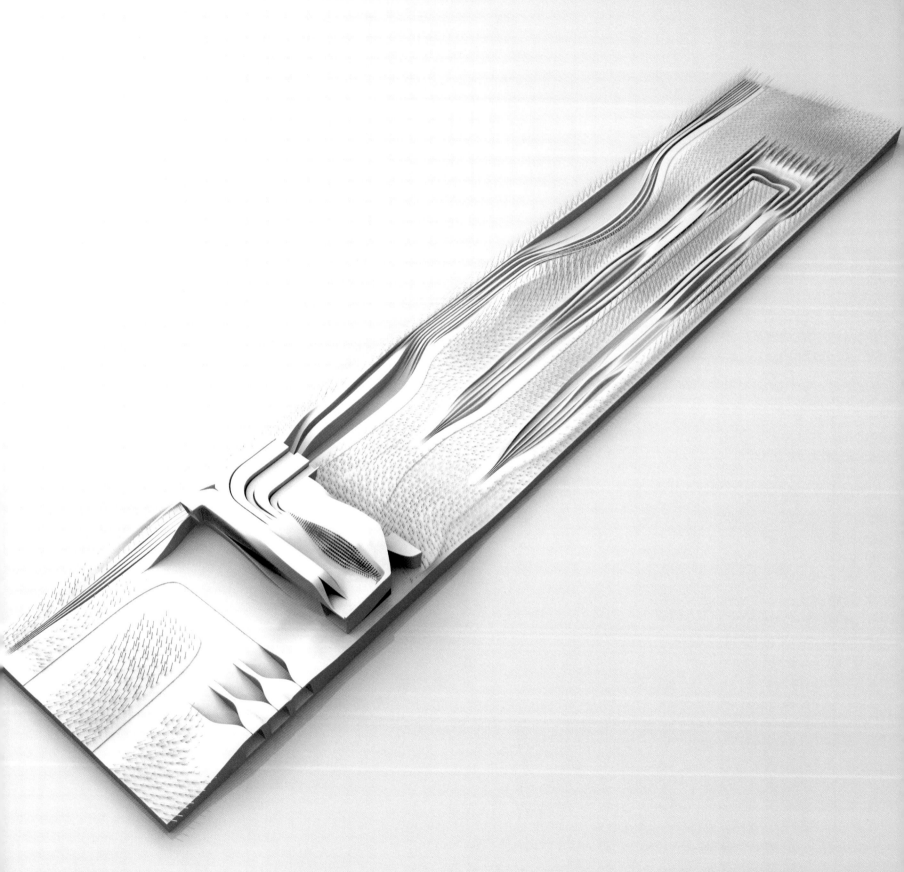

Detail Model. Relationship of House to Retaining Wall and Landscape

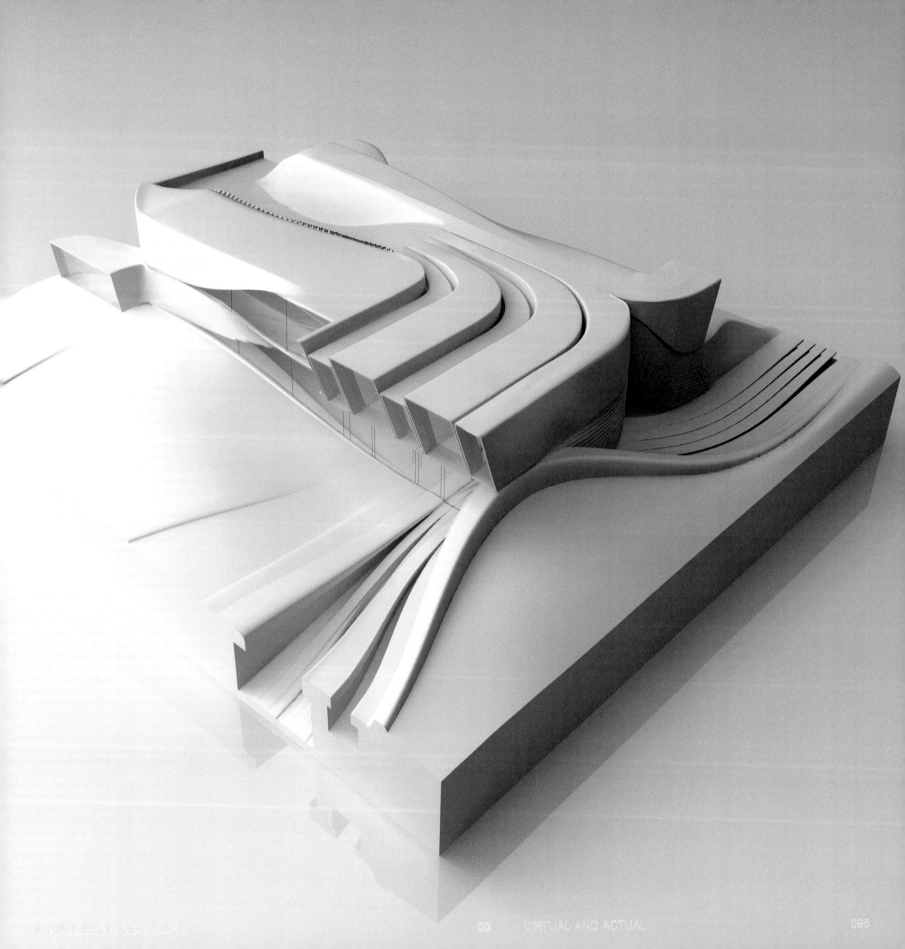

Detail Model. Vehicular and Pedestrian Entry

Sectional Model

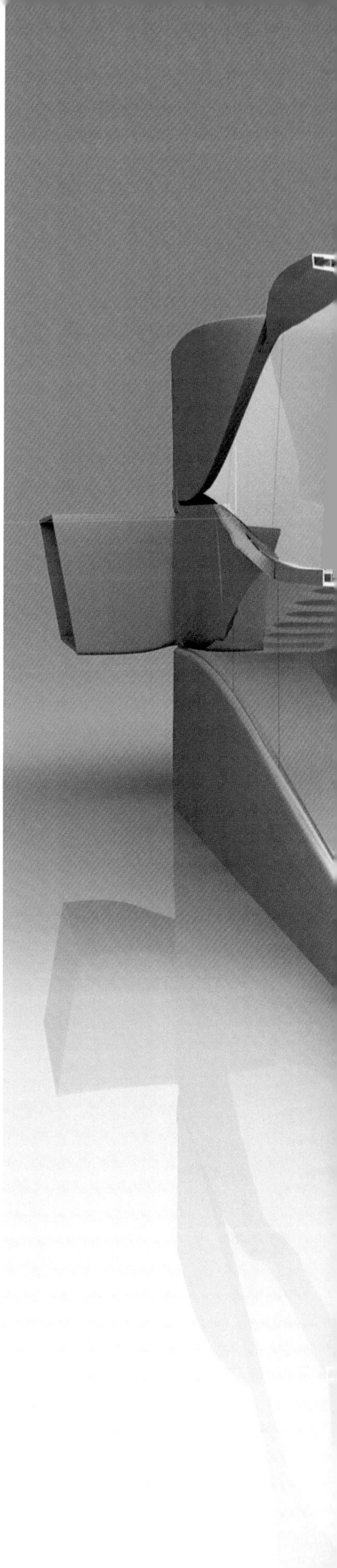

Site Plan. Continuity of Landscape Topography with the Residence

A   Soft Landscape
B   Irrigation Well or Retention Pond
C   Irrigation or Retention Channels and Catwalk for Fashion Shows
D   Play Area

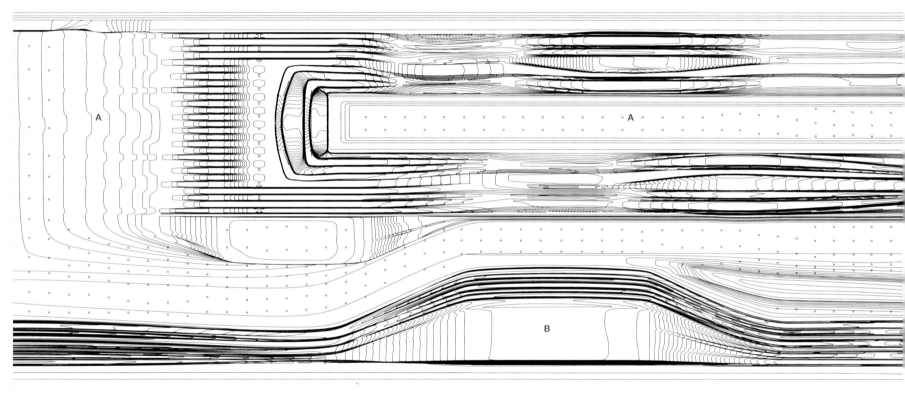

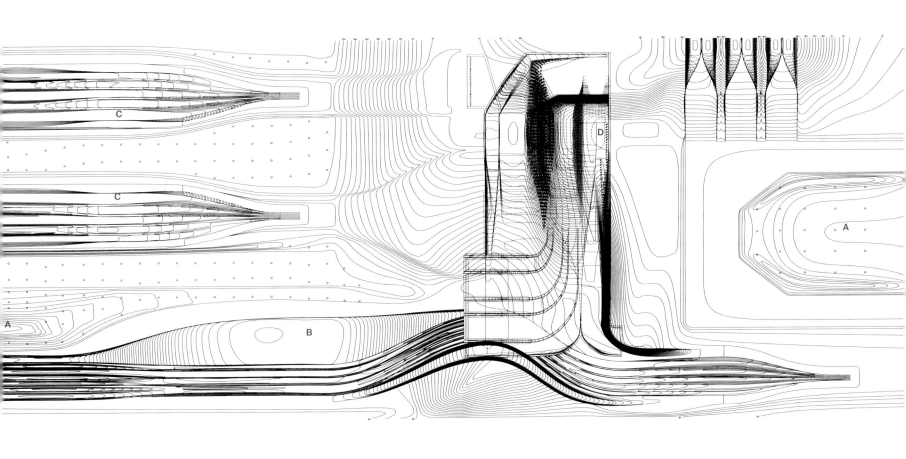

Elevation Drawing. Sectional Relationships between the Retaining Wall and Landscape

Elevation Drawing. Sectional Relationships between Vehicular Parking and Landscape

A   Top of Roof, +9 meters
B   Second Level, +4.2 meters
C   Entry Level, +0.0 meters
D   Parking Garage, –1.75 meters
E   Channel, –0.5 meters

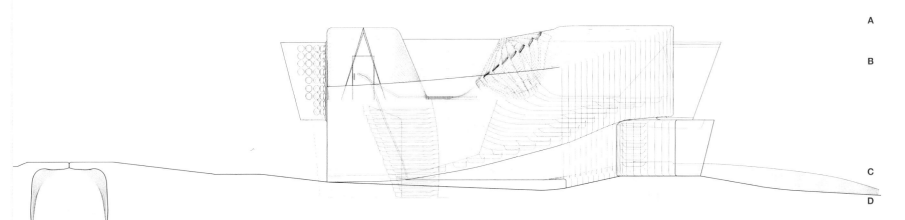

A

B

C

D

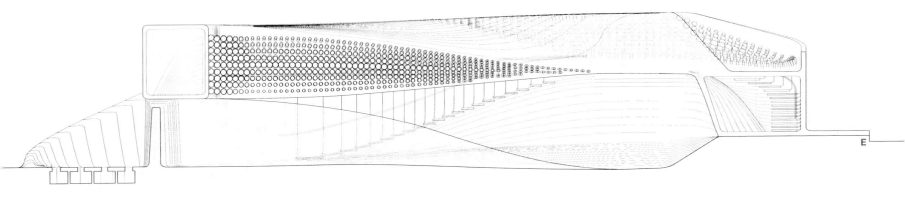

E

Entry View

Exterior Detail. Light Openings

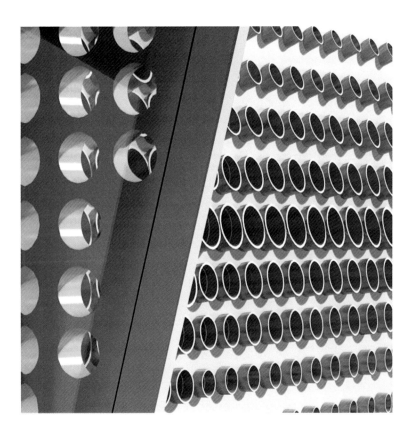

Exterior View

Interior Stair Detail

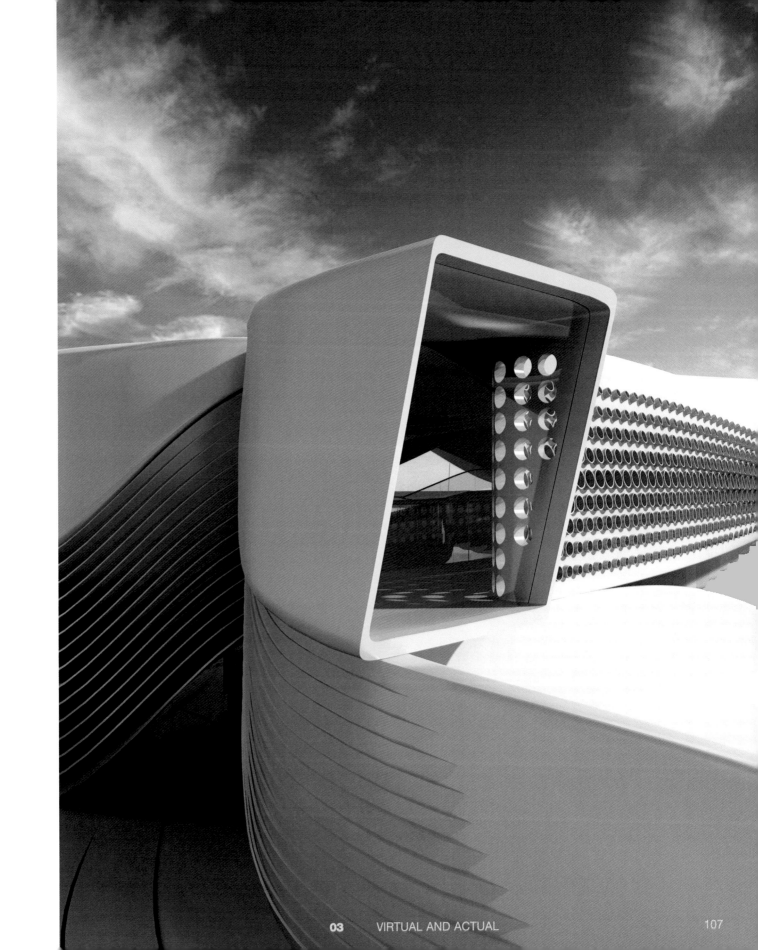

Exterior View from Landscape

Exterior View

First Level. Inflected Surface for Entertaining

Second Level. Inflected Surfaces for Sitting and Leaning

Second Level. Lighting Gradient

PROJECT 04 VARIABLE POROSITIES

Library for the Information Age
Karachi, Pakistan, 2003

The new Library for the Information Age fulfills at least three
roles: first, it serves as a local cultural and educational venue for
the residents of Karachi, Pakistan's largest city. Second, it forms
a network and shares a collection with similar libraries in
Islamabad and Lahore. Third, it functions as the base of a global
information network about Pakistan. Located at an intersection
in the heart of Karachi, the new 325,000-square-foot library sits
opposite two similar-sized hotels. The building will house both
paper-based and digital media, including a book collection,
spaces to access an online databank, and facilities for public
uses and functions.

We were interested in how the library's combination of uses and
media could shape the design of the project. Two factors were
considered in particular: first, the different modes of information
transfer that occur in the library—both the one-way
transmissions entailed by the act of reading and the two-way
exchanges that occur during electronic and person-to-person
interactions—and second, the difference in the weights of
paper-based versus electronic media. We decided to use a
dynamical system generated in the computer to incorporate
pressures based on these two factors as well as several site-
related influences. As we developed the system, it became clear
that the goal was to provide a range of spatial environments or
"porosities" that would allow visitors to interact with digital and
traditional media in different ways. The library's spaces should
change in response to shifting patterns of use and information
exchange. Furthermore, by extending these dynamic
interchanges to the building's landscape and beyond, the library
could become a vital force in the city.

The dynamical system was structured with several pressures
corresponding to the site, building, modes of communication,
and weights of media. High-intensity pressures related to the
dynamics of the surrounding neighborhood were located
towards the perimeter of the site and a low-pressure system
corresponding to the library's public spaces was placed in the
center. An additional pressure system based on gravity loads,
or the weight of media, influenced the flow from high to low

pressures. Through the modulation and adjustment of the pressure systems, several trajectories developed. The trajectories were applied to a field of inverse-kinematic (IK) chains organized in a three-dimensional grid over the site. A pattern of contractions and expansions between the layers of IK chains emerged. As the technique began to yield desired spatial outcomes such as sectional variations and pockets of space compatible with the different media types, the pattern of inflections was actualized into a formation. The curves of the IK chains were used as the basis for generating the formation's various surfaces.

The actualized[12] library retains the heterogeneous features generated during its development in its spaces, surfaces, circulation, and relationship to the city. The compressions and expansions between the IK chains yield a multiplicity of spaces with different degrees of porosity: areas formed through expansion are flexible and open to the city while compressed zones are more static and closed. Digital media and computer stations are placed in the more porous areas, which are located toward the center of the building. Porous zones contain a greater number of inflections, affordances,[13] and indeterminate and unprogrammed surfaces, and can be reconfigured easily to provide spaces for lectures and performances. Traditional paper-based media such as books and magazines are located in the more compressed areas near the exterior of the building, constraining the amount of light entering the building. Areas affiliated with traditional media, such as reading rooms, are located near the stacks. The compressed spaces are organized in more static arrangements of shelves and study carrels that have fewer potential uses.

The patterns of expansion and compression also shape the use potentials of specific surfaces in the library. Surfaces formed by expanded curves feature a greater number of inflections. The inflections can be activated in a range of ways: some allow users to sit and gather in groups while others permit visitors to lean and watch a performance. Other inflections become lighting patterns in the ceiling. In contrast, surfaces formed by compressed curves are smooth and flat, and provide for a more limited range of uses: they serve as the floors supporting the book stacks and reading rooms. The precise affordances activated emerge through use. If one person leans on one of the curved surfaces in the new media spaces, his or her action will influence how others congregate nearby.

The library incorporates a range of circulation routes that allow users to move at various speeds. Large-scale openings permit visitors to wander slowly through the porous public and new media areas. A faster circulation path comprised of smaller-scale openings links the book stacks and reading rooms. An elevator provides the fastest path between levels, allowing users to shortcut the other routes. The provision of these different speeds of circulation affords visitors a range of ways to negotiate the library's differentiated spaces. Together, the circulation paths generate a

dynamism in the space of the library similar to the intensity of urban life.

The building's affordances extend out to the surroundings. The building and its landscape comprise a continuous concrete surface inflected to offer a range of uses. On the south side of the site, a bench merges seamlessly into a set of ponds. A series of channels provide drainage during the summer monsoon season. Elsewhere, the inflections of the channels are used as beds for planting grass. Runoff from the drainage channels is collected in retention ponds and is released slowly to the grassy areas. In the parking area, the paved surface opens to provide shade for cars; other inflections in the road surface serve as speed bumps. The paved surface's affects can also be activated in other ways: teenagers can skateboard on the speed bumps or children can sit on them.

The library incorporates a range of uses and interfaces within a seamless and variably porous formation. The building affords users numerous shifting ways to interact with digital and traditional media and encourages visitors to learn new techniques for inhabiting and occupying space. The dynamism of the unfolding relationship between the library and user extends beyond the walls of the building to activate the landscape and the city. By providing numerous potentials for groups to form and intermingle, the library stimulates conversations and exchanges. Such interactions arouse users' awareness of their connections to each other and to the city and give rise to affects that ripple through the metropolis and beyond.

Dynamical System Composed of IK Chains

A   Areas of Expansion
B   Areas of Contraction

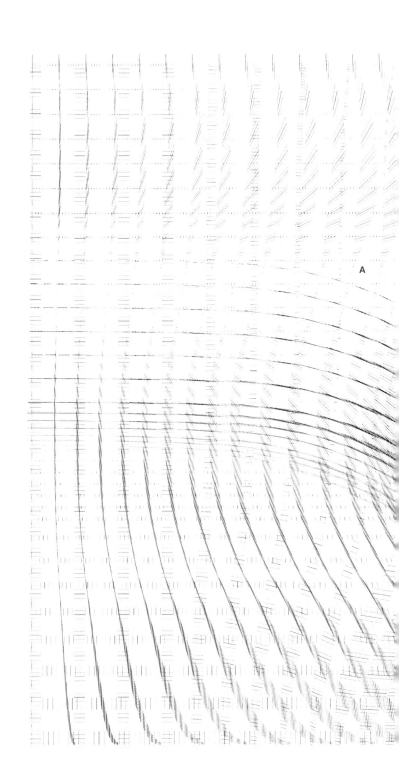

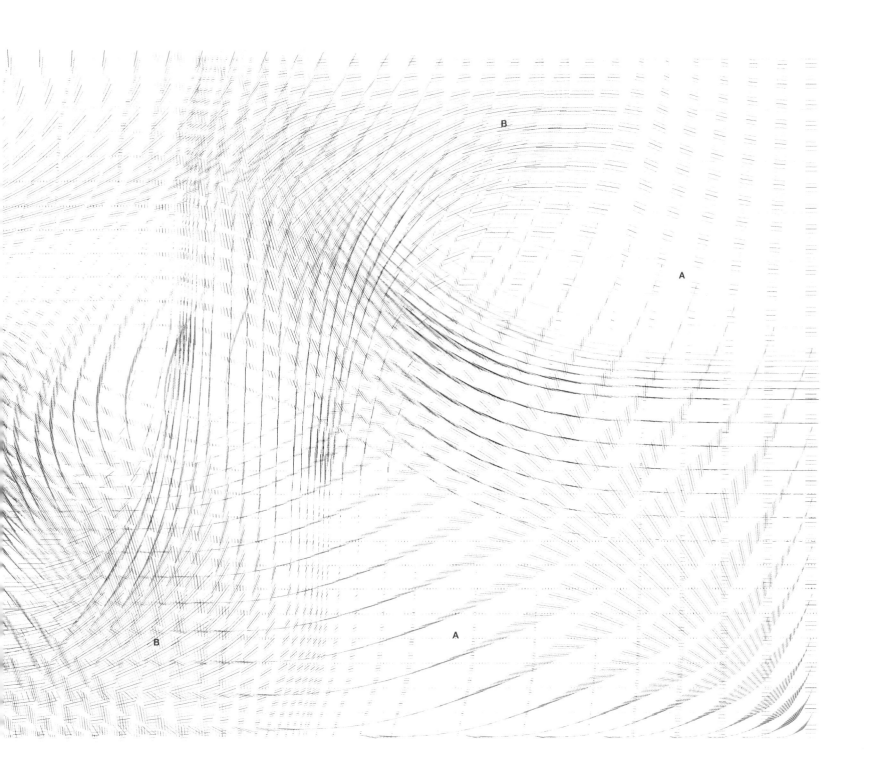

Site Model

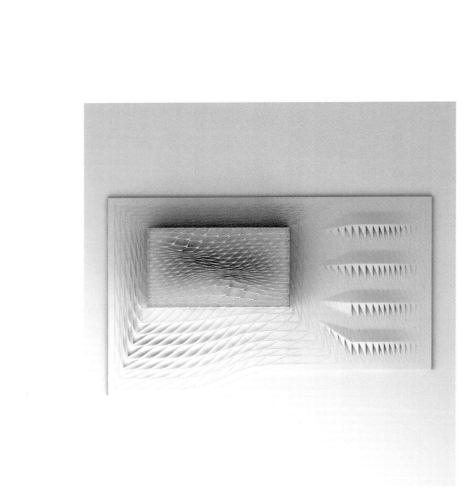

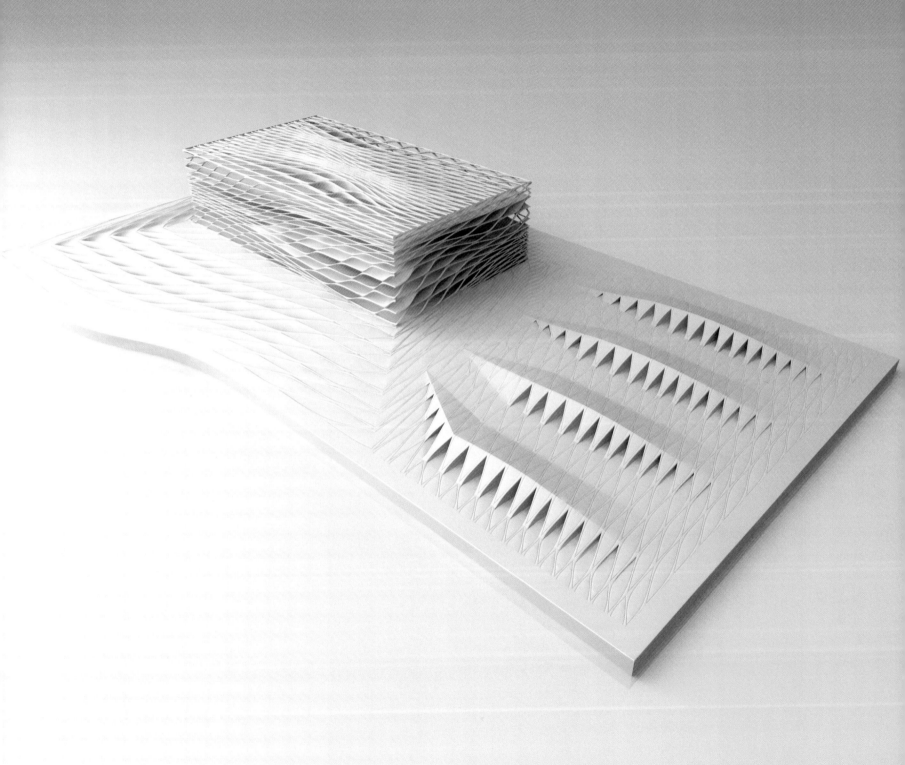

Longitudinal Sectional Model. Relationships among Porous Public Spaces, Compressed Book Stacks, and Intermediary Reading Rooms

Third Level Plan

A   Porous Spaces for Performances
B   Intermediary Spaces for Reading Rooms
C   Compressed Spaces for Book Stacks

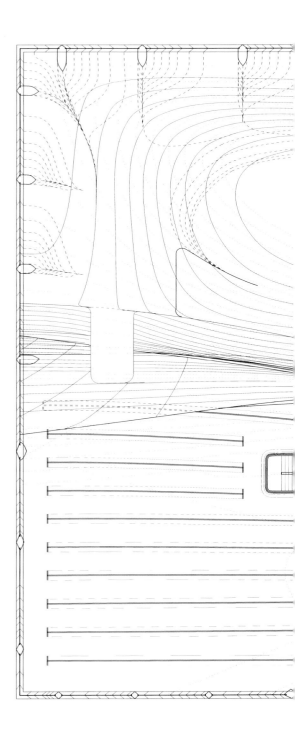

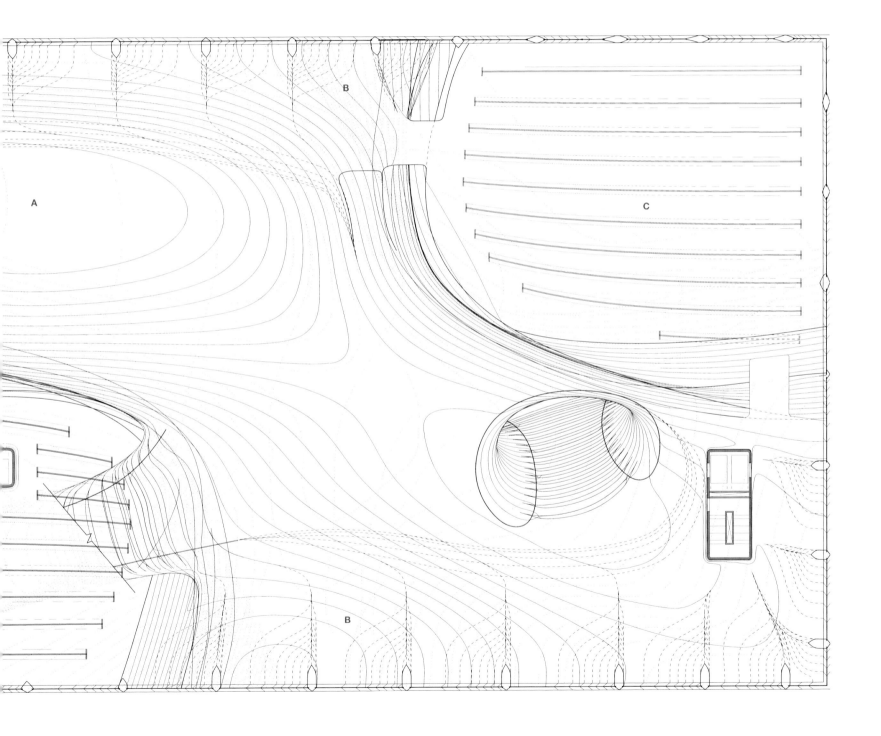

Exterior View

Facade Detail

View of Roof Café

Detail View, Continuity between Facade and Landscape

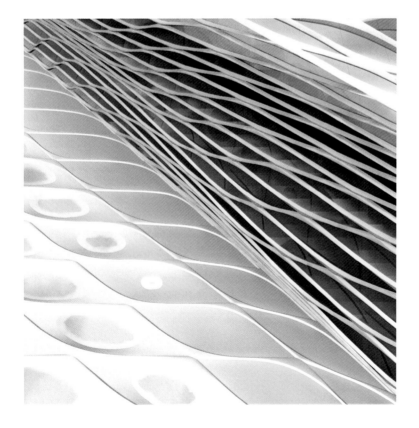

Exterior and Interior View

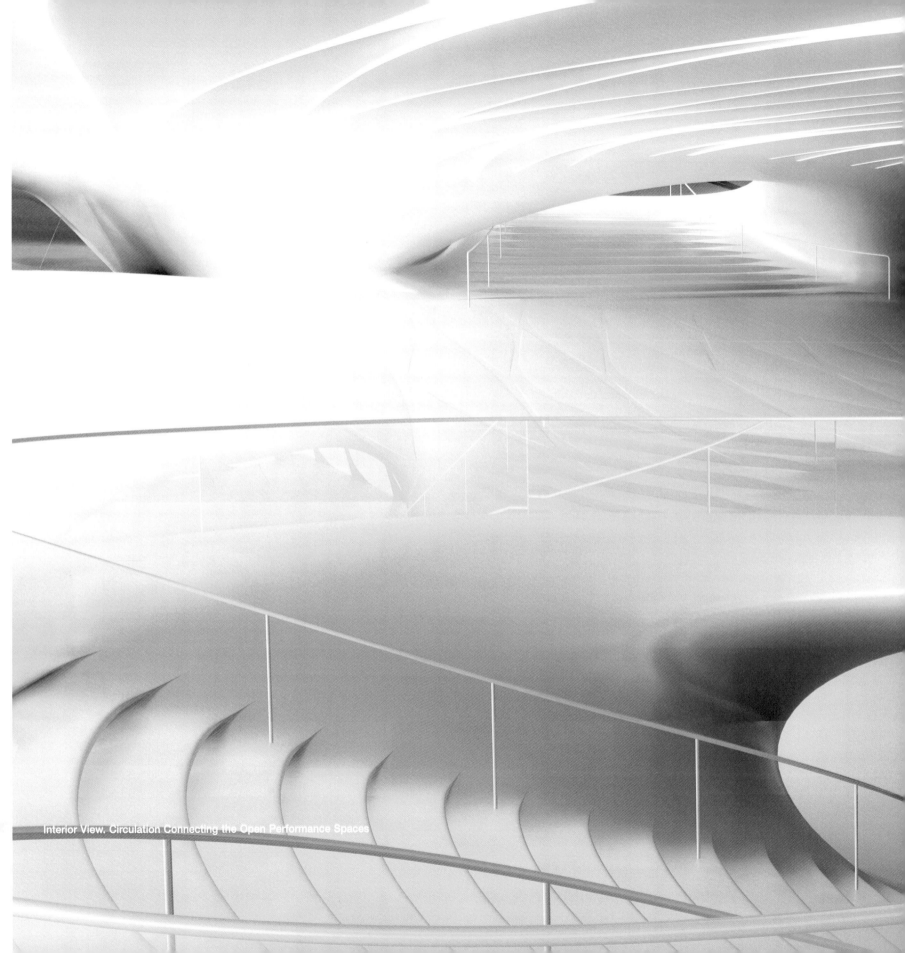

Interior View. Circulation Connecting the Open Performance Spaces

01   Dorothea Olkowski, *Gilles Deleuze and the Ruin of Representation* (Los Angeles: University of California Press, 1999), 122.

02   Reyner Banham, "A House is Not a Home," in *Architecture Culture 1943–1968*, ed. Joan Ockman (New York: Columbia Books of Architecture, 1993), 374.

03   Jacques François Blondel stated in 1749 that all the major types, their programs, and their characters were specified: "Public markets, fairs, hospitals, and military buildings would be masculine; garden structures, rustic; prisons, terrible." See Anthony Vidler, "The Idea of Type: The Transformation of the Academic Ideal," in *The Oppositions Reader*, ed. K. Michael Hays (New York: Princeton Architectural Press, 1998), 439–457.

04   Elizabeth Grosz, *Architecture from the Outside* (Cambridge, Mass.: MIT Press, 1999), 130.

05   Manuel Delanda, *Intensive Science and Virtual Philosophy* (London: Continuum, 2002), 54.

06   Ibid., 235.

07   Grosz, 129.

08   Ibid., 6.

09   For discussion on actualization, refer to page 077.

10   For discussion on affordance, refer to page 138.

11   For discussion on affects, refer to pages 136–137.

12   For discussion on actualization, refer to page 077.

13   For discussion on affordances, refer to page 138.

14   For discussion on formation, refer to page 078.

04 AFFECTS AND EFFECTS

Architecture generates cultural change by intensifying and inflecting existing modes of inhabitation, participation, and use. To accomplish this, architecture must become more responsive, engaging in a relationship of mutual feedback with its users and contexts. In other words, it must contain *affects*[01] —the capacity both to affect and to be affected. Affects differ from effects, which generally imply a one-way direction of causality: a cause always precedes its intended effect. Affects, in contrast, suggest a two-way transfer of information and influence between a formation or work of architecture, and its users and environment.

To illustrate the difference between affects and effects, it may be helpful to consider an example: the construction of a street curb. The cause of this action is to separate pedestrian circulation from automobile traffic; the effect is a raised ledge in the street. There is a direct, intentional relationship between cause and effect. Other unplanned outcomes may also occur, however. A child may sit on the edge of the sidewalk, using it as a bench. Skateboarders may utilize the sectional shift in the road as a recreational surface. These uses do not result directly from the cause. The potential for these other activities are the curb's affects—its capacity to affect users' behaviors and to be affected, or transformed, through evolving uses. Affects reside in an object or formation's features—in the differences of form, texture, and material that constitute it. In the case of the curb, a difference in geometry gives rise to its affects. These affects are then activated through interaction with specific users.

While all works of architecture arguably have affects, certain projects are more prolific than others. Technological practices are interested in producing *affective formations*—works of architecture that maximize their affects and hence their responsiveness to users and contexts. Below, I explain how designers generate affective formations through temporal techniques and how affects become activated through use. Three examples drawn from contemporary architecture illustrate the development of affects within a formation at a range of scales—from the texture of surfaces to the dimensions of a building to the scale of the city. Last, I suggest how affects can catalyze a feedback loop between designers, techniques, formations, users, and proliferating cultural effects. By cultural effects I do not mean direct targets of causes but, rather, unintended outcomes that have the power to instigate further ripples in culture.

AFFECTIVE FORMATIONS

Affects, and hence affective formations, are generated through techniques. Once produced in the course of a project's development, affects can shape the technique itself and thus influence the final form of the object. To understand this, one needs only to think of a technique such as the application of paint to a surface: the deposit of pigment creates an affect that is embedded in the resulting differences in color and texture. This affect then directs and inflects subsequent strokes. Each brush stroke affects and is affected by the one after it. The painter adjusts his or her technique in response to affects generated during the act of painting, thus influencing the shape of the final formation or work of art. Form is not imposed on the affects; rather, affects inform the process of formation and vice versa. Techniques, affects, and form respond to and alter one another, constituting a feedback loop.

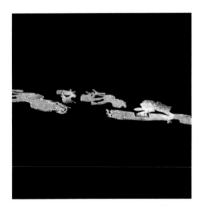

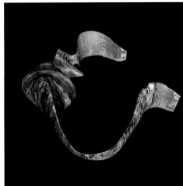

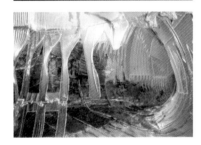

Predator, Wexner Center, Columbus, Ohio. Fabian Marcaccio, 2001
Predator, Wexner Center, Columbus, Ohio. Greg Lynn FORM, 2001
Predator, Wexner Center, Columbus, Ohio. Greg Lynn FORM, 2001

Although there are several ways to create affective formations, the methods emphasized in this book are temporal techniques—specifically, generative methods such as dynamical systems and transformational procedures such as shape-shifting. As I explain in Chapters 02 and 03, temporal techniques contain elements of virtuality—a space of potentialities that can lead to the generation of unexpected effects. Affects form a crucial link in the capacity of the virtual to instigate new outcomes and behaviors in users. They are specific instances of the virtual. Using techniques that consciously highlight the role of the virtual therefore increases the likelihood of producing an affective formation. Virtualities, and hence affects, develop under specific conditions of temporal techniques: in dynamical systems, affects arise in the differences between rates of change in pressure trajectories, while in transformational procedures, affects emerge from the interaction between pressures applied directly to an object and the object's own material resistance. In both cases, the greater the differences in the pressures, the greater the degree of transformation in the surface or object. And the more intense the transformations, the more affects are contained within the formation. Affects are embedded in the formal properties produced by transformations generated as part of temporal techniques—for example, elongations that result from stretching, bent surfaces created by folding, and openings caused by tearing.

Each transformation generates multiple *affordances*—specific properties of a formation that indicate how one can interface with the formation.[02] The empty space within an open doorway is an affordance: it indicates the possibility of moving across the threshold. Affordances are essentially all the "action possibilities" latent in the environment; they are objectively measurable, and exist independently of an individual's ability to recognize those possibilities. Affordances activate the affects produced through temporal techniques. For example, an affect generated through stretching a surface may afford an area for sitting; one created through tearing may yield a staircase. As affects vary across the surface of an object, so do the affordances, or possible interfaces. Affordances are triggered by and vary with the capabilities of the user. For example, a set of steps with two-foot-high risers does not afford the act of climbing to a crawling infant. Affordances thus change with use.

Affective formations enable and encourage individuals to form new kinds of connections with spaces. Because they are produced from intense processes of transformation, affective formations often present unfamiliar landscapes to users. Affects within the formation cause users to sit, walk, or sometimes engage in less prosaic activities. Each individual can be said to contain his or her own affects, which interact differently with the affects contained in the formation. As each person responds uniquely to a formation, he or she activates certain affordances within the object. His or her behavior then influences the reactions of adjacent users. Once one person has sat, others may sit—or they may be prevented from doing so. Small groups may form; some people may find themselves perched on a surface that is higher than is customary, others sitting on areas that are much lower than normal. Individuals may find themselves in new relationships with others. The affective formation instigates inventive modes of inhabitation by users, perhaps changing their conceptions about what constitutes an appropriate surface for sitting, or what it means to sit in a group. If this group moves and other individuals come along and repeat the process, the resulting arrangement might be completely different, as the affects contained within the new participants activate another set of affordances and affects in the formation.

Context also plays a crucial role. An affective formation placed in the environment of a museum may give rise to one kind of reaction: visitors may assume it is a piece of artwork and stand at an appropriate distance. The same object placed in a nightclub will likely inspire entirely different responses and uses. A formation set in the countryside will generate different interactions than if it is placed in the city. The goal for the designer is not to fully comprehend and control all the complexities of affects and affordances but, rather, to inflect formations with affects, coaxing forms and occupations in useful directions.

AFFECTS AND TEMPORAL TECHNIQUES: *PREDATOR*

Affective formations are often technique driven. A case in point is *Predator* (2001), an installation created by Greg Lynn in collaboration with the painter Fabian Marcaccio for the Wexner Center in Columbus, Ohio. By developing the project through a sequence of techniques, affects were embedded at several scales—from the inflections of the formation's surfaces to its overall form to its spatial conditions. These affects were only activated through the interaction of visitors.

Lynn began by using a dynamical systems technique to magnify the contrast between the installation and its context in the gallery. Using the software Maya, he transformed a set of modeling objects by interfacing them with a dynamical system containing intense pressure differences. These pressure differences generated trajectories with different rates. The differences between these rates acted upon the objects, inflecting,

expanding, and contracting them, generating affects which, in turn, influenced the process of transformation itself. The resulting formation retained many of the affects generated in the dynamical system in the form of various surface curvatures and inflections. Marcaccio, the painter, then applied another technique, brushing pigment onto a canvas surface. Each brush stroke embodied a pressure of unique intensity. The interactions between the aggregate pressures contained in the strokes and in the viscosity of the paint generated affects, which shaped the form of the painting. The two techniques were combined by digitally scanning and projecting Marcaccio's painting onto Lynn's transformed meta-objects in the computer. Lynn then used another set of techniques to manipulate this hybrid formation, digitally shrinking and wrinkling the surface along the brush strokes. The surface was shredded into strips that were pulled apart and then fused back together to create gill-like openings of various sizes. The surface of the meta-object thus acquired all the differences embedded within the painting. The surface was then unfolded in the computer and translated into three-dimensional tool paths that were fed into a computer numerically controlled (CNC) routing machine. The router molded 250 foam panels with crenellations corresponding to the digital model. The panels were then covered with vacuum formed plastic sheets laser-printed with Marcaccio's painting. The vacuum forming entailed heating the plastic sheets, a process that changed their molecular structure and allowed them to bend precisely around the foam. The deformation of the plastic created affects that then shaped and were shaped by subsequent surface transformations. In the final step of the installation process, Marcaccio dripped a coat of paint directly on the surface of the formation. Again, the paint responded to the affects generated in previous transformations—such as those embedded in the deformed texture of the plastic—and produced its own affects—by changing the opacity of the surface, for example.

Each technique in the process built on the one before it and inflected the one that followed. Affects accumulated with every transformation. At each stage, differences and evidence of the process were retained, and these manifested themselves in the final formation. Once *Predator* was installed in the space of the Wexner Center, these affects became activated through interaction with users. The complex *mélange* of colors, textures, curvatures, and degrees of opacity created a formation that appeared almost alien, provoking unique responses in each individual. Approaching the installation, the splitting of the surface created openings that afforded the possibility of walking into the piece itself. The scale of these openings granted adults and children different ways of entering. If visitors did not see the openings, or did not want to go inside, these affordances lay dormant. Affects embedded in the texture, thickness, opacity, and color of the paint activated different sets of affordances in response to the movements of each user. As the visitor walked through *Predator*, the affordances and affects shifted continuously.

The reaction of visitors to *Predator*, while initially limited to private or collective responses within the gallery space, may yet yield catalytic effects. Just as people once were alarmed by the thinness of the Eameses' curvilinear chairs, those who enter the space of *Predator* may be unsettled. These reactions may lead some to reconsider what distinguishes a work of art from architecture, or how one defines beauty. The affects embedded in *Predator* may produce responses in visitors that feed forward to the modification of norms in visual culture in the future. Fifty years from now, surface texturing and the embedding of vibrant colors may become mainstream within architecture.

AFFECTS AND AFFORDANCES: RESI-RISE SKYSCRAPER

Affects also play an important role in Resi-Rise (1999–), a high-rise housing tower designed by Sulan Kolatan and William MacDonald of KOL/MAC Studio. Kolatan and MacDonald conceived of Resi-Rise as a kind of "vertical urbanism" rather than as a building. The components of the project included a frame or matrix of three-dimensional lots, built to the maximum allowable zoning envelope, and customizable pods that would be inserted into the lots. Individuals leased different-sized pods based on their financial capacity and desires. The overall shape of the building would change as units were sold or rented. It was expected that the top and bottom units of the structure, considered the most valuable from a real estate perspective, would sell first, and that the rest of the building would be filled in gradually.

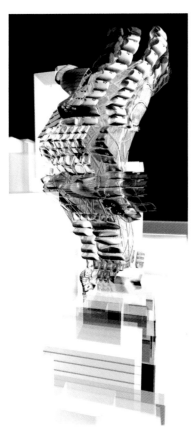

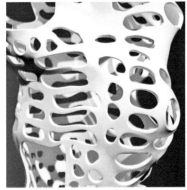

Resi-Rise Skyscraper, New York City, US, KOL/MAC Studio, 1999–
Resi-Rise Skyscraper, New York City, US, KOL/MAC Studio, 1999–

The architects began by creating a dynamical system in the computer that integrated pressure differences correlated to factors such as economics, site, zoning envelope, views, and adjacencies between units. To model the frame of the Resi-Rise, Kolatan and MacDonald used a malleable mesh, a method that could integrate local differences within a cohesive structure and thus was appropriate to the repetitive cellular structure of a residential tower. The pods were modeled as meta-objects, entities that have zones of influence enabling them to inflect, and to be inflected by, adjacent meta-objects. These zones of influence enabled the meta-objects to register affects. The field of pressures, mesh, and meta-objects mutually shaped and modified one another, generating affects with each transformation. The differences between rates of trajectories expanded, contracted, pushed, and pulled the meta-objects. With each transformation, affects were registered at the scale of the meta-object as well as the entire tower.

In the actualized project, the affects generated in the formation's transformations create affordances at a variety of scales: within each pod, in the relationships between pods, between the pods and tower, and in the overall tower itself. At the scale of the individual pod, deformations of the exterior surface inflect the interior, affording residents various possibilities to interact with the inside surfaces—from lying to sitting to planting on them. At the scale of the relationship between pod and tower, the affordances change in response to local and global conditions. For example, in an economic downturn, a majority of occupants may opt for smaller units, giving the tower a finer-grained appearance; in periods of growth, the desire for larger units might lead to a more expansive overall effect. The sale of one unit affects the next. For example, if a prospective buyer wants an urban unit—one located closer to other pods—he or she might purchase a unit near other recently sold lots. If the buyer prefers a more suburban atmosphere, he or she might opt for a unit far from other pods. The density of the tower might also change, activating different affordances: a high vacancy rate could result in pockets of the tower being filled with open parks in place of pods, affording a more suburban organization and altering the relationships between neighbors. The local changes also shape structural affordances in the whole. As pods of varying weight and volume are occupied or emptied, the vertical and lateral loads operating on the building change, and structural affordances in the overall mesh are activated as needed.[03] The relationships contained within the formations are not fixed but adapt to the behaviors of the users and to external conditions. Resi-Rise contains innumerable affects that, through interactions with users and environmental conditions, have the potential to generate catalytic effects both small and more significant. These effects may yet feed forward, cascading to generate changes in the relationships between neighbors, the design of residential towers, or even practices in real estate development.

AFFECTS AND CATALYTIC EFFECTS: GUGGENHEIM MUSEUM, TAICHUNG

To understand how a building can contribute affects to its immediate urban context and beyond, we can look at Zaha Hadid and Patrik Schumacher's proposal for the Guggenheim Museum (2003), in Taichung, Taiwan. Hadid and Schumacher conceived of the museum as a changing event space that would respond to, and be influenced by, the city. The building is part of an urban assemblage that eventually will include a new town hall, city assembly, and national opera house. To design the museum, Hadid and Schumacher used transformational techniques to manipulate a volume modeled as a network of interconnected curves and points. Pressures correlated to various site conditions such as adjacent roads and buildings were applied to the volume, instigating a series of distinct transformations to the overall form. The gradients between these different transformations produced affects, which were embedded in inflections in the form and surfaces of the building—specifically, its bends, cleavages, and openings. For example, the surface over the lobby space was pushed and pulled, giving rise to skylight openings. The production of each affect shaped and altered the next. The final formation was thus a hybrid of numerous transformations, all of which produced affects that were retained in the fluidity and dynamism of the actualized project.

The formal inflections and differences generated by the transformational techniques produce the museum's affordances. Areas that are more curvilinear provide more affordances than areas with zones with sharper transitions between surfaces. These affordances provide capacities for interaction between the building and individual users, but also between the museum and the city. The actualized formation blurs the boundary between landscape, building, and canopy. At one end, the building has been bent, affording a 50-meter canopy over a nearby road. At the other end, ramps emerge out of the ground to link the city with the museum spaces, affording urban dwellers an unprecedented degree of fluidity in interacting with the building. The ramps split, giving passersby an opportunity to experience the space of the museum without even entering or, alternatively, allowing them to walk into the galleries or to pass through to the park on the other side of the building. The lobby features an

Guggenheim Museum, Taichung, Taiwan. Zaha Hadid with Patrik Schumacher, 2003

Guggenheim Museum, Taichung, Taiwan. Zaha Hadid with Patrik Schumacher, 2003

Guggenheim Museum, Taichung, Taiwan. Zaha Hadid with Patrik Schumacher, 2003

internal landscape of rising and falling forms that allows it to be read as an extension of the city. The galleries also express an openness to the visitor, encouraging passersby who might not have entered the exhibition spaces to do so. Thus, the architecture affects users, potentially altering their behaviors.

The building may be altered by its users in ways that are difficult to predict. The precise affordances activated depend on the visitor. The openness of the museum's public spaces may encourage individuals to use them as surfaces for recreation, commerce, or performance. The formation also generates affordances at the scale of the city, opening the museum to a wide variety of new public uses and altering the typical relationship between interior public space and exterior urban fabric. Groups may spontaneously congregate there for weekly picnics—as they do in the plaza of the Hong Kong and Shanghai Bank and other public areas in Hong Kong. What distinguishes the Guggenheim in Taichung from the bank, however, is that the former is created with temporal techniques, which generate far more affects than the conventional design processes that were presumably used to create the bank. Of course, the bank contains affects that generate unexpected effects as well: after all, the adoption of the plaza underneath as a public gathering space was probably not an effect intended by the designer. However, the Guggenheim, with its more complex and differentiated surfaces, affords users a greater degree of flexibility and variability, thus multiplying the potential modes of occupation. Different from the bank, the designers of the Guggenheim intended to build variability and open-endedness into the formation itself, and used techniques specifically designed to accomplish these goals by generating affects. In the museum, the actions of one user change the possibilities of occupation for all other users, activating affects that ripple across the whole, and ensuring that the form of the gatherings will differ from week to week. In contrast, the weekly gatherings at the bank are fairly constant in their shape and organization: they have become more functions of habit and custom than of invention. The exact consequences of affective formations are emergent and therefore cannot be known in advance. What is certain, however, is that the transformational techniques employed in the making of these formations result in surface inflections and changes that have the capacity to inspire a wide range of uses. Formations are not only backdrops against which life occurs, but are critical in structuring life and, in turn, are structured by use.

Affects connect formations with their uses and contexts. They are a pivotal link in the feedback loop of architectural innovation: technological practices use temporal techniques to create formations with affects. These affects are manifested in affordances that are activated by users, generating responses that may feed forward to instigate broader cultural effects. The effects that arise from affective formations may primarily be visual, as in the case of *Predator*, or visual, social, and economic, as with Resi-Rise. Or they may alter the relationships between city dwellers, public institutions, and the city, as does the Guggenheim in Taichung. The magnitude and reach of the project's influence depends on a cascading of effects from individuals to small groups, from groups to communities, and from communities to nations or even international bodies. Affects accelerate a formation's capacity to incorporate the influences of users and contexts and to shape its environment. In a sense they are the catalysts that allow architecture to become catalytic.

PROJECT 05 MIGRATING COASTLINES

Residential Housing Tower
Dubai, UAE, 2004–

The 45-story, 450,000-square-foot residential tower overlooks the city of Dubai and the Arabian Gulf on one side and the desert on the other. Located on Sheikh Zayed Road—the main thoroughfare connecting Dubai and Abu Dhabi, the project attempts to engage Dubai's status as a regional economic hub and as a haven for foreign nationals seeking to invest abroad and to hedge political unrest at home. By catalyzing exchanges with both its residents and the larger city, the building aims to facilitate a series of migrations, whether human, economic, or architectural.

To incorporate the myriad economic factors and site relationships into the design, we generated a dynamical system model in the computer. A high pressure was located on the side of the site facing the city and a low pressure on the side of the desert, to instigate flows from the city toward the desert. Pressures correlated to the ocean and desert views were also inserted. In addition, high pressures were located near the top and bottom of the tower and lower pressures in the middle, in order to generate a flow that would activate the center—the section of the building typically considered least desirable from a real estate perspective. As the structure and intensity of the various pressures were modulated, a feedback loop formed. Differences in pressures generated trajectories that affected[04] and were affected by one other, responding to and redirecting flows in the system. The pressure system was then applied to a series of two columns of 45 stacked particle fields. The behaviors of the particle fields were constrained to tend toward three desirable conditions: privacy between units, maximization of views to the surrounding landscape, and the provision of several emergency exit paths. The pressure systems combined with the particles' own behavioral constraints, causing the fields to stretch, compress, twist, and gradually organize into an emergent pattern. Particles moved to the perimeters of the formation, leaving empty spaces in the center. The twisting of the particle fields generated the tower's undulating profile—a vertical coastline marking the flows and migrations within the system. In addition, the middle floors of the building became compressed or shorter in height. As these new organizational patterns emerged, we saw new possibilities for the economic development of the middle section of the tower. The formation was actualized and the affects generated from the dynamical system were developed further in metric space.

The actualized[05] formation consists of two contiguous 45-story buildings that fuse, shedding their individual identities. Each particle field becomes a story in the tower and is developed into a variable module consisting of concrete, glass, and portions of a concrete structural core, elevator shaft, and emergency exit stairs. In aggregate, the variations between the modules produce the dynamic shape of the overall tower. The exterior glass walls are inflected, some curving outward and others remaining flat. The windows are clad in heat-sensitive low-iron glass that exhibits differing qualities depending on the location of the sun and amount of heat gained on its surface. The structural modules also twist over the height of the building, altering the load-bearing capacities of each floor. The elevator core stays roughly in the same position between floors, but the emergency stairs are torqued to maximize their potential utility.

The inflections in the building's envelope and cores cause the interior spaces to compress and expand from floor to floor. The plan of each level is unique. On floors where the emergency stairs and elevator core are close together, the space in between may be used for storage; on the floors above, as the two cores move farther apart, the interstitial area grows larger and may afford a dining space. The compression of the middle levels leads to units that have lower ceiling heights and are generally smaller and more affordable, alleviating the potential undesirability of the apartments on these floors. The units in the tower thus avoid the repetition and sameness typical of high-rise residential buildings. Apartments in the building range from studios to four-bedrooms and vary in size from 1,000 to 5,000 square feet. However, the complex inflections of spaces, room sizes, ceiling heights, and apartment organizations makes it impossible to reduce units to descriptions such as "two-bedroom." Instead, each apartment affords[06] a range of conditions and possibilities for occupation that expands the developer's options for marketing the units.

The relationships between structure, emergency stair core, and unit change not only between floors but also in response to the unique affects[07] of each user. For example, the curvature of the exterior glass windows generates affects that change in relation to the perspective of inhabitants and passersby moving within or past the building. As the building's envelope and spaces shift, twist, and rotate, they produce migrating affects in perception and use. At a larger scale, these perceptual and occupational affects may attract other foreign nationals to purchase units in the building. Hence the formation has the potential to inflect local migration patterns and to be transformed by changing occupancies.

The building also contains affects in relation to its site. Several features at the base of the tower may serve to draw commerce away from Sheikh Zayed Road and toward the desert, possibly increasing the value of the land behind the tower and producing another migrating coastline. Amenities at the base include ponds that create a cool environment and power outlets that may facilitate the gathering of markets. The exact outcomes generated by such affordances depend on the specific behaviors of users. The intention, however, is to provide the potential of shifting economic exchanges and openness towards the desert.

By suggesting a new approach to selling real estate—in terms of qualities and potentials of space rather than simply square footage, the design of the tower may influence how developers build and market condominiums in the future. The formation comprises a series of migrating coastlines that reflect and shape the resettlement patterns of its residents—specifically, their attempts to gain residency in the UAE by purchasing real estate in Dubai. Finally, the tower inflects the local economic conditions of Sheikh Zayed Road, potentially shifting the relationship between the desert and the city.

Dynamical System. Particle Fields

A   Emerging Vertical Coastline
B   Migratorial Patterns of Particles

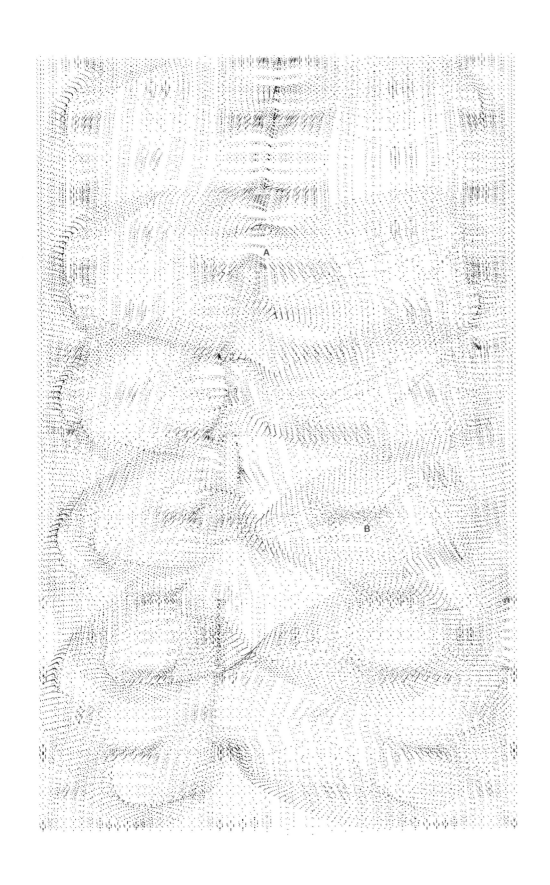

Aggregated Variable Modules

Sectional Model Coastlines

Sectional Model Detail

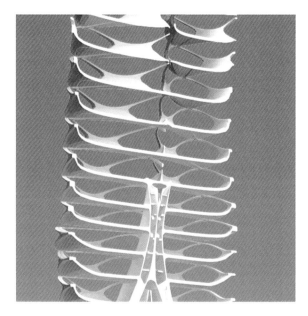

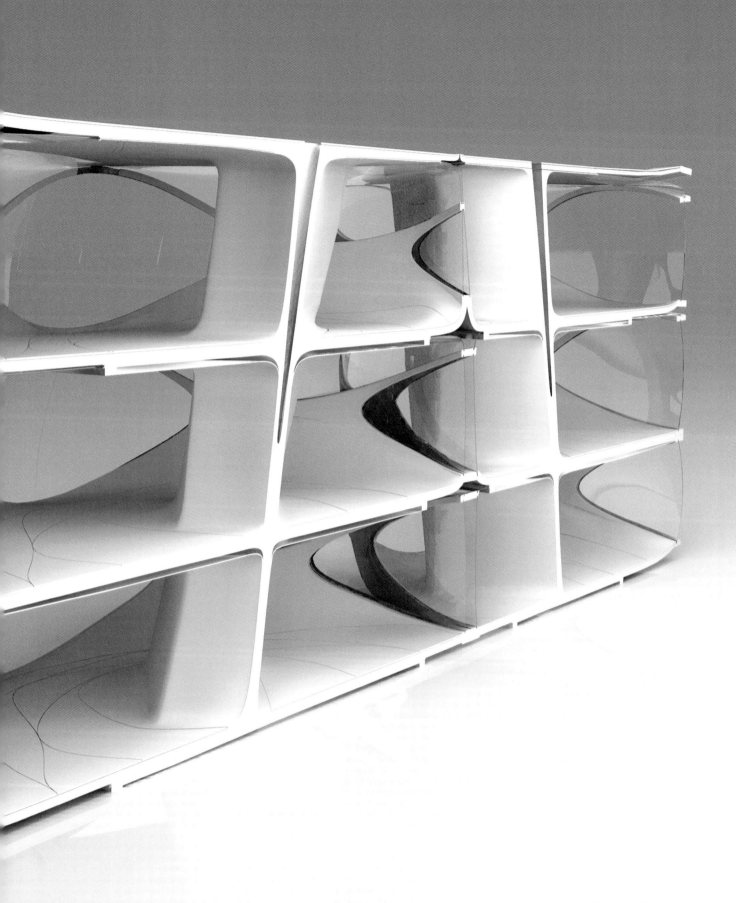

Elevation Detail

Elevation

A   22nd Level, +76.5 meters
B   21st Level, +72.5 meters
C   20th Level, +68.5 meters
D   19th Level, +64.5 meters
E   18th Level, +60.5 meters
F   17th Level, +56.0 meters
G   16th Level, +52.0 meters
H   15th Level, +47.0 meters
I   14th Level, +43.0 meters
J   13th Level, +39.0 meters
K   12th Level, +35.5 meters
L   11th Level, +32.0 meters

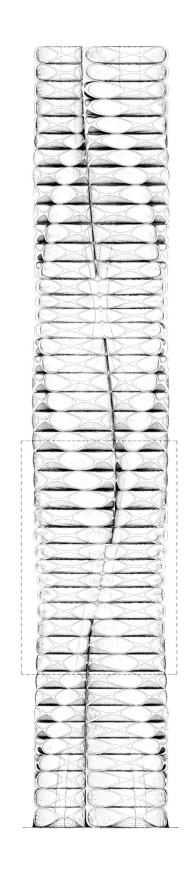

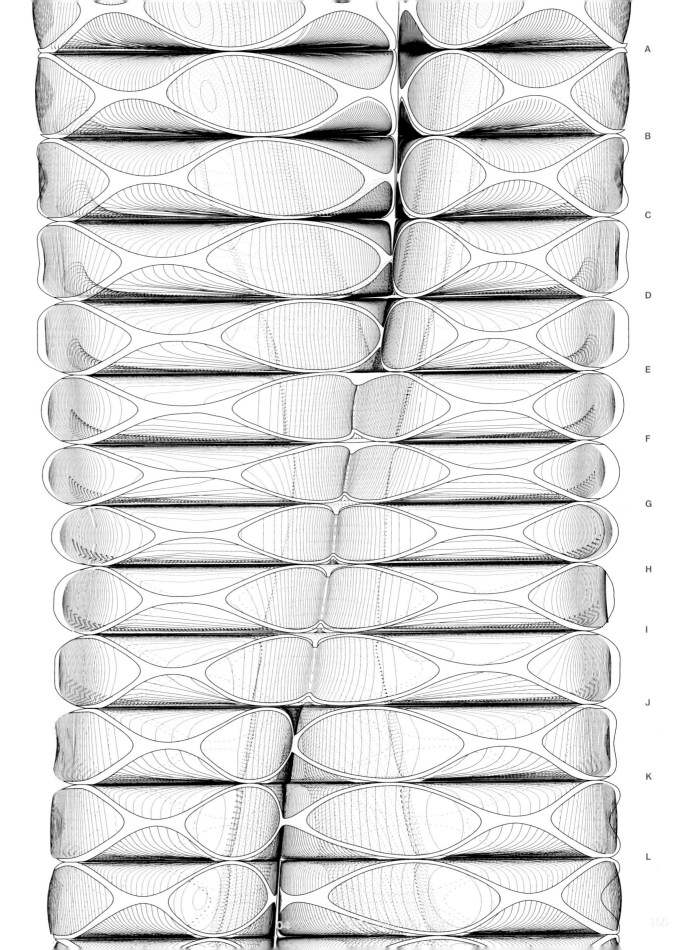

Unit and Plan Variation Extreme 2

Unit and Plan Variation Extreme 1

A   Keyed Elevator Access
B   Emergency Stairs
C   Kitchen Area
D   Bathrooms

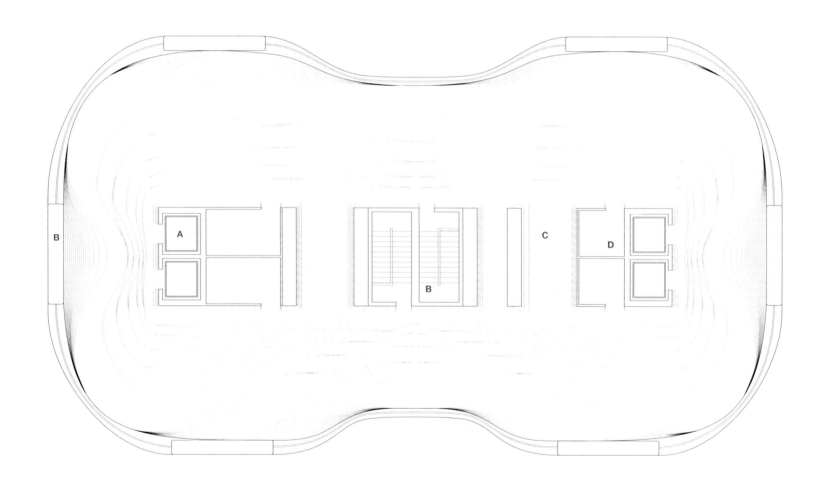

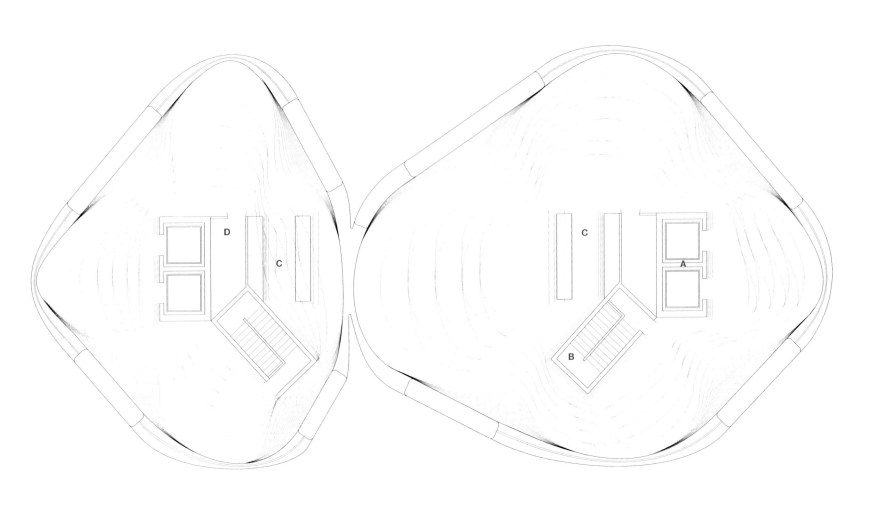

Exterior View

Site Model. Sheikh Zayed Road

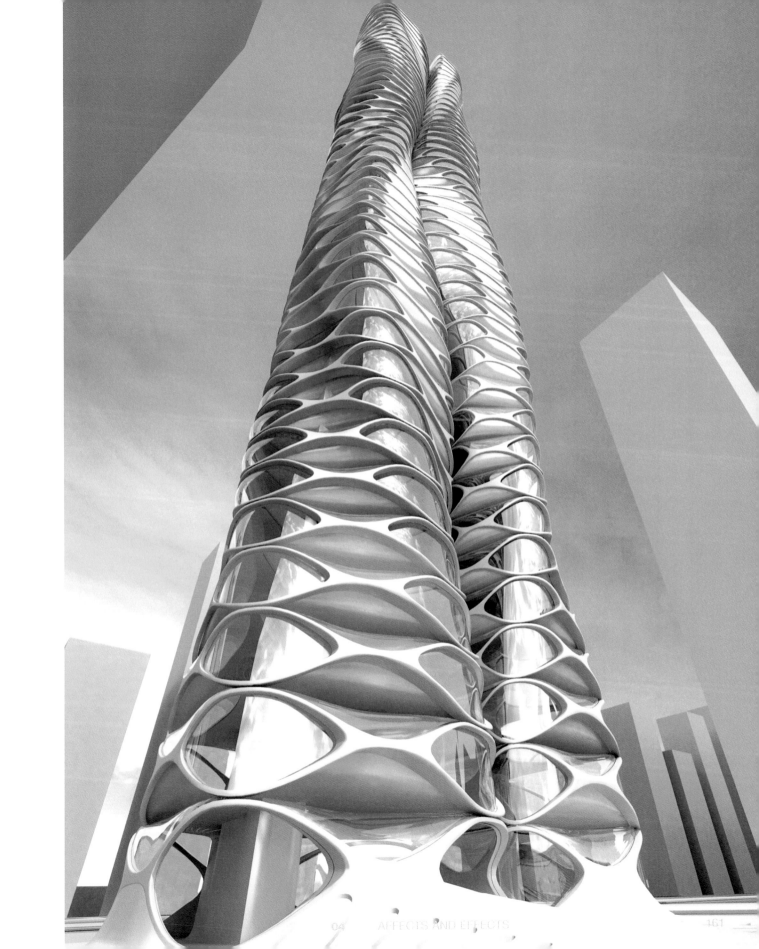

Interior View. Extreme Variation 1

Exterior View

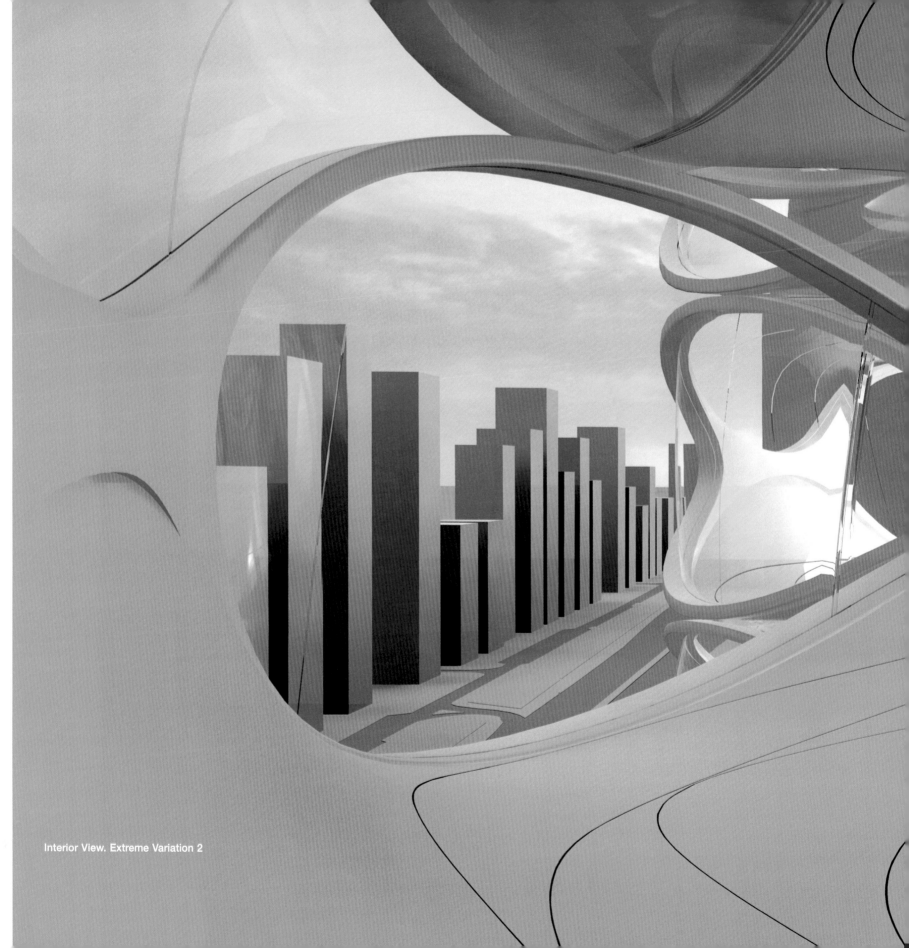

Interior View. Extreme Variation 2

Exterior View

PROJECT 06 INFLECTING ORGANIZATIONS

Commercial Office Tower
Dubai, UAE, 2004–

The 38-story, 463,000-square-foot office tower is located in the commercial marina district of Dubai. The man-made marina, strategically sited on the Arabian Gulf, will encompass 30 million square feet of new residential and commercial towers, including the developments Dubai Internet City and Dubai Media City. Recent statutory changes allowing foreigners to buy and own property in Dubai have led to a soaring demand for new residential and commercial space. Since many new businesses fail in their first year, however, office space in particular tends to turn over quickly. The aim of the project therefore is to help occupant companies to survive by maximizing affects[08] between firms and their employees and between companies. Increased interactivity will lead to the generation of new ideas and collaborations, lowering the risk of failure. Thus, the building may catalyze larger economic, urban, and regional effects.

We started by locating the tower and parking in order to take full advantage of the site. The tower was placed to the northeast and the parking to the northwest of the long, rectangular lot. The building provided views of a lake towards the north and west and of the Arabian Gulf towards the east and the south. We then created a dynamical system model in the computer, structured with two types of pressures: a high-intensity oscillating pressure that would function as an economic attractor to draw businesses and a series of low pressures correlated to local organizations within the building. As the system was activated the movement between the high and low pressures produced affects and feedback loops which, in turn, influenced and reorganized the system. Once the pressure differences were maximized, we placed a matrix of meta-objects inside the zoning envelope and studied the results. The intensity of pressures and density of the meta-objects were adjusted until patterns of organization began to emerge: the meta-objects formed groups, expanding and contracting to generate differences in the heights between floors. Meta-objects also began to accumulate at the perimeter of the project, creating a series of shared spaces. When we were satisfied that the emerging patterns met our aims—to develop a new organization of office spaces on the interior and unique facade features on the exterior—the formation was actualized and developed further in metric space. Each meta-object was traced three dimensionally with curves that were connected to form surfaces.

The actualized formation of the tower contains numerous affects from its generation—within its spatial organization, circulation, facade inflections, and its relationship to the landscape. Transformations in the building's surfaces result in diverse spaces, including interstitial voids on the perimeter that connect two or more floors and that serve as shared conference rooms. The offices are not completely segregated but, instead, comprise an open, undulating landscape. The building's organization does not conform to the conventional hierarchical office typology with executive suites located at the perimeter of the building and open support spaces at the center. Instead, the design fosters dynamic relationships between spaces and users. As businesses or departments of companies come together in spaces such as the shared conference rooms they may influence one another, exchange ideas and practices, or even merge into new hybridized entities. Companies are not limited to predetermined needs or organizations. The flexible organization of the tower allows firms to combine, expand, downsize, or sublease, catalyzing affects and leading to unpredictable economic outcomes.

Circulation through the tower is similarly flexible and varied. Some paths link offices within a floor while others connect multiple floors and conference rooms. The provision of diverse routes helps to maximize the building's possible uses and hence its economic viability. For example, a circulation route between floors may allow one office to spill into another. Businesses are not necessarily limited to the spaces they have rented but can possibly leak into other floors. Interconnectivity between spaces maximizes the possible scenarios for occupation. Large organizations can disperse themselves throughout the building, or small organizations may occupy pockets of space with the potential to expand as needed.

The building's envelope also contains variations that produce diverse affects. The envelope is made of glass and a mixture of poured-in-place and prefabricated concrete panels. The varying combinations of concrete and glass produce a range of lighting effects that influence the layout of workstations and shape affordances within each space and floor. Sunny zones may provide spaces to gather while darker areas offer a place for computer workstations. The fenestration pattern attempts to maximize the range of possible working environments and the economic potential of the businesses that inhabit the building.

Affects are also contained in the relationship between the tower and the surrounding landscape. Transformations in the surfaces of the tower continue into the parking garage to create ponds that cool both the garage interior and the building facade, resulting in lower energy costs. The landscape's inflected surfaces contain affordances[09]

that may be activated by users as places to sit and eat lunch; when full, the ponds may allow employees to swim. Inflections in the surfaces are also used as speed breakers for cars or as ramps to access the various parking levels.

The transformations in the tower thus create affordances at every scale of the formation. Spaces and surfaces allow for flexible and inventive uses depending on the behaviors of their inhabitants. Individuals can develop new use patterns and associations within the office landscape, generating feedback and potentially multiplying the building's affects. The tower's spatial affordances may engender new relationships within and between companies, maximizing their chances for survival and producing positive effects on local and regional economies.

Model

Model without Facade

Plan. Shared Conference Areas

A Lobby, +0 meters
B Bathrooms, +0 meters
C Conference Area, +1.5 meters
D Conference Area Above, +3.5 meters
E Coffee Area, −1 meters
F Conference Area Below, −3 meters

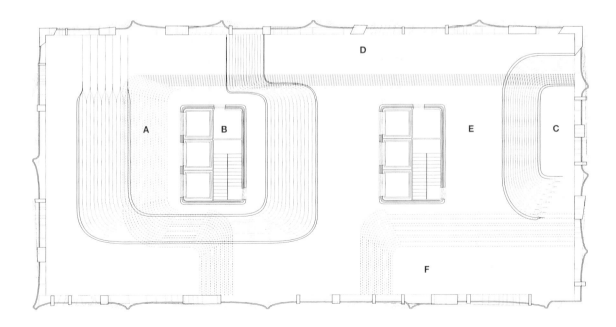

Exterior View. Facade Variation

Aerial View

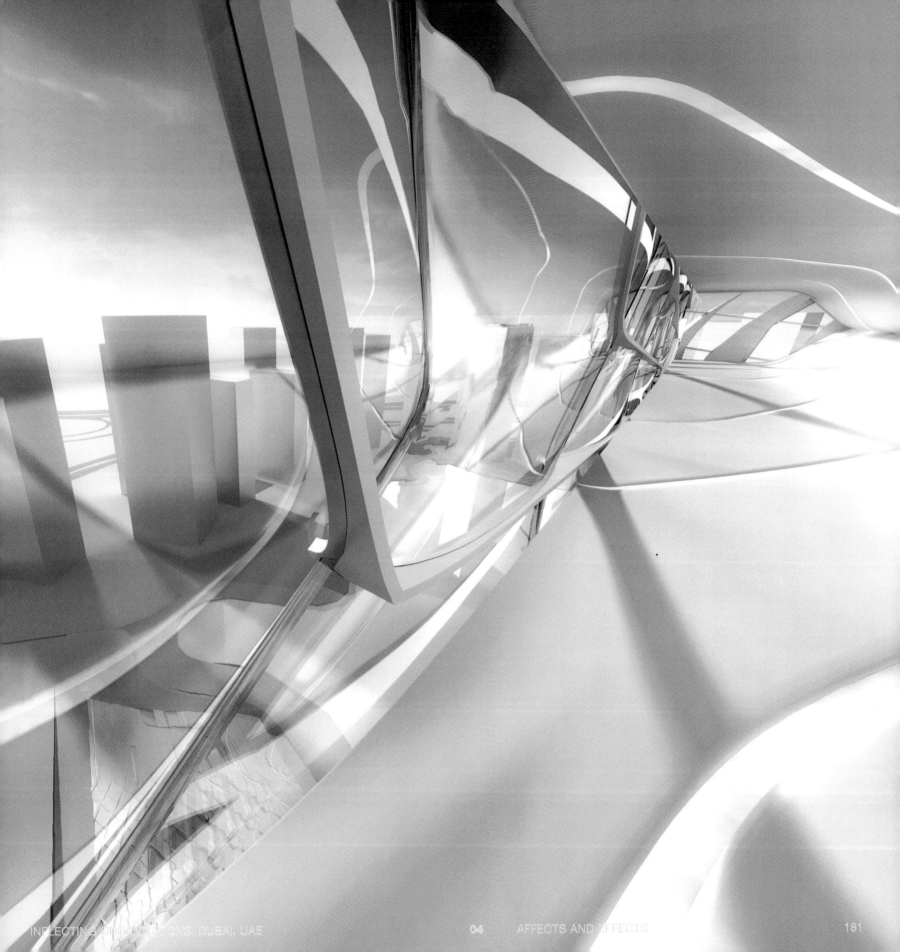

Conference Room View

Lobby View

01   Gilles Deleuze in *Difference and Repetition* (New York: Columbia University Press, 1994).

02   The concept of affordances was first introduced by psychologist James Gibson in 1966. He explored the idea more fully in *The Ecological Approach to Visual Perception* (1979; Mahwah, New Jersey: Lawrence Erlbaum Associates, 1987).

03   The tower's structural frame comprises two cross-linked, basket-like rings, constructed of prefabricated fiber-reinforced composite components. The frame is wrapped with a membrane that provides a degree of enclosure as well as lighting and ventilation. The pods are lifted into place and secured to the frame and to adjacent pods. The pods are made of hybrid monocoque shells that include partially transparent areas. Prefabricated plumbing, ventilation, electrical systems, and communications networks are embedded in the shells of the pods.

04   For discussion on affects refer to pages 136–137.

05   For discussion on actualization refer to page 077.

06   For discussion on affordance refer to page 138.

07   For discussion on affects refer to pages 136–137.

08   For discussion on affects refer to pages 136–137.

09   For discussion on affects refer to pages 136–137.

10   For discussion on affordance refer to page 138.

05 FEED FORWARD: NEW TECHNOLOGIES AND FUTURE TECHNIQUES

In order to stay at the forefront of cultural developments, technological practices must continually reinvent themselves, creating techniques to exploit new technologies. Innovative techniques are the hallmark of technological practices. At the beginning of the twenty-first century, for example, forward-thinking architecture offices have devised methodologies to incorporate computer-based generative algorithms into the design process and computer numerically controlled (CNC) milling technologies into architectural fabrication. These developments are not only altering the forms of contemporary architecture but also giving design a new-found efficacy. New techniques enable designers to generate catalytic formations that are singularly interactive and that feed forward to the invention of more technologies and techniques, thus furthering the development of architecture and other cultural spheres.

Of course, no technique is guaranteed to produce architectural innovation. As I explain in Chapter 01, however, architects can invent techniques with specific features that are more conducive to generating catalytic cultural effects: namely, they incorporate feedback from the environment and user, destabilize standard methods, and are process driven and interdisciplinary. The first characteristic must be stressed in particular: feedback loops are the engines that drive the innovation. Techniques that generate and respond to feedback are more likely to change and evolve, eventually giving rise to new technological and cultural developments.

Since innovation is an emergent phenomenon, it is impossible to predict the precise pressures that will shape architecture in the future. We can, however, try to identify promising technologies that may lead to the development of new techniques. In this chapter, I briefly outline some criteria by which designers can evaluate potential new tools, and look at a few examples of up-and-coming technologies that may transform architectural design and fabrication in the years ahead.

SELECTING NEW TECHNOLOGIES

New architectural techniques are developed in one of two ways: the first is by modifying existing methods within the discipline—including some of the techniques discussed in this book. Methodologies using dynamical systems, for example, might be refined by adding real-world material properties to the models. This would allow architects to test and potentially hybridize material behaviors during a project's development, increasing the range and specificity of the affects produced. The temporal techniques elaborated in this volume are still in their infancy. With further development, they will continue to alter the production of architecture in the short and long terms.

The second strategy for developing new techniques is to identify promising technologies in other fields that can be adapted for architectural uses. This raises the question: how do designers evaluate which technologies offer the most promise? The answer is simple: they look for technologies likely to yield techniques with the characteristics outlined earlier. Hence, architects should be particularly interested in recent developments in other fields that facilitate the incorporation of feedback from the user or environment in real time. A technology that is responsive at a local scale will likely give rise to techniques that generate feedback at a larger scale. As I explain in Chapter 04, feedback occurs through the creation of affects—capacities within a formation both to affect and to be affected. Affects operate in the relationship between a formation and its users but also between techniques and culture at large—that is, techniques generate affects in culture and vice versa. Designers should be attentive to technologies with the potential of destabilizing existing architectural practices. Such technologies may have already provoked transformations in other fields, or they may contain features that differ markedly from conventional architectural methods. Technologies that tend to be used through repetition and experimentation are of interest because they may give rise to process-driven techniques, ones that work from the bottom-up and contain a generative potential. Finally, although the borrowing of a technology from another field guarantees that a resultant technique will be interdisciplinary, architects can look especially to technologies that themselves incorporate multiple disciplines and ideas. Inventions that arise from diverse sources tend to contain greater potential for crossover uses than ones developed in isolation.

To illustrate these ideas, in the following sections, I offer five examples of technologies that fulfill the above criteria and speculate on their potential to instigate new architectural techniques. Drawn from the automobile, robotic fabrication, and sail manufacturing industries, and the material sciences, all five technologies have the potential not only to transform and integrate design and fabrication but also to generate more affective—and hence catalytic—works of architecture.

VIRTUAL CRASH TESTING AND DESIGNING WITH FEEDBACK

One of the most promising new technologies that effectively incorporates feedback is virtual crash testing software, an innovation developed in the automotive, aeronautics, and aerospace industries. In virtual crash testing, a responsive digital environment based on a dynamical system model realistically simulates material behaviors and feedback in a collision. In the testing environments used by the automobile industry, for example, every component of the crash scene is modeled and specified, including the form, dimensions, material, and weight of

Virtual Crash Testing Simulation. ESI Group, 2002
Virtual Crash Testing Simulation. ESI Group, 2002

each car part. The physics of each material, whether metal, composite, or glass, is taken into account. The technology registers the relationships between the various scales of the car's organization, from the overall vehicle to a door to a piston, all within a single animated model. Every conceivable environmental parameter is specified: the speed of travel, the wetness or dryness of the road, the coefficients of resistance of various surfaces, and the weight, gender, height, and age of passengers. If a rider is pregnant, the computer adds this information to the model. Once all of these parameters are established, the software can test a car's behavior in any imaginable scenario, and evaluate the effects of a collision on the vehicle and its passengers.

Virtual crash testing enables automobile manufacturers to iteratively experiment with, and fine-tune, a product to achieve desired performance levels. The ability to study numerous scenarios and conditions in the computer progressively eliminates the need for physical prototypes.[01] Because virtual crash testing environments incorporate multiple factors such as context, material, form, structure, and use in one model, they enable the car's various components to be developed simultaneously: the structure of the chassis and the car's cladding can be tested and designed at the same time. Virtual crash testing thus allows automobile manufacturers to collaborate more closely with the makers of individual parts. Perhaps the most important aspect of this technology, however, is that it yields emergent effects—ones that unfold through a process. The complex interaction of the environment with the material attributes of the vehicles in a collision—a state far from equilibrium—produces outcomes that cannot be predicted: the precise damage to the vehicle at several scales, for example, or the effects on the passengers. The usefulness and validity of the results depends on the comprehensiveness and accuracy of the system's parameters. Additionally, virtual crash testing allows designers to see the systemic effects—in other words, the impact of environmental and other pressures on a system as a whole.

The incorporation of virtual crash testing technologies into architecture may give rise to several new techniques for design. Architects can use the software to iteratively test formations and their feedback with users and environments in a single model. Factors such as material behaviors and resistances, structural capacity, user responses, and environmental conditions can be adjusted precisely and feedback generated in real time. Thus, designers can study how specific inflections of forms, spaces, and materials influence the production of affordances and affects in users— for example, how a particular formal transformation shapes the tendency of groups to spontaneously assemble. Environmental conditions such as wetness or dryness and their effects on users' interactions with a space can be tested. The capacity of virtual crash testing environments to assimilate myriad factors within a single model may allow the work of engineers, cost estimators, and fabricators to be integrated more rapidly. The effects of a change in structure on fabrication time and cost could be calculated almost immediately. Most significantly, techniques derived from virtual

crash testing might allow architects to access unpredictable outcomes. The aim is to develop more responsive design, testing, and manufacturing environments in which the development of form, material, structure, and user responses occur simultaneously, yielding emergent formal and spatial conditions.

CONTOUR CRAFTING AND TESTING MATERIAL AFFECTS

While virtual crash testing offers promise primarily as a design tool, contour crafting, a technology developed at the University of Southern California, holds potential for profoundly altering the way structures are built. Originally developed to fabricate large-scale parts for the automotive, aerospace, and building construction industries, contour crafting combines advances in the field of robotics with three-dimensional printing technologies, also known as rapid prototyping, developed at the Massachusetts Institute of Technology in the late 1980s. Unlike rapid prototyping, which is a slow process used primarily for small-scale fabrication, contour crafting can generate structures as large as houses in comparatively short periods of time. In contour crafting, a computer-controlled machine pours and shapes a claylike material in layers until a complete structure is formed. The machine is composed of a robotic gantry attached to an extrusion nozzle and two trowels. As material is extruded through the nozzle, the trowels can create smooth, accurate surfaces of any curvature.

Since contour crafting relies on computer-controlled machines to carry out fabrication, it opens the door to future techniques that may reduce the gap between digital design and building methods. By linking a manufacturing technology such as contour crafting with digital design tools and environments, architects may soon be able to experiment with techniques that incorporate real-time feedback from design into fabrication and vice versa. For example, designers might begin to explore the effects of different pouring techniques and variations in the consistency and mixture of materials. Changing the wetness of pours between layers might produce drips, smooth planes, or other surface affects; combining translucent and opaque substances in the same pour might generate other interesting visual affects. These affects can be tested simultaneously in the computer and actual fabrication

IGES Hyposurface. Mark Goulthorpe dECOi, 2000

IGES Hyposurface. Mark Goulthorpe dECOi, 2000

IGES Hyposurface. Mark Goulthorpe dECOi, 2000

A series of robotic arms respond to digital inputs, either programmed or interactive. This system is suggestive for future production techniques that may be guided through interaction and variability.

environments: feedback between the two realms can give rise to more unpredictable affects. Such potential techniques are process driven, relying on iterative modulation, experimentation, and feedback between the design and manufacturing environments. They contain an emergent potential, as each round of design and fabrication has the potential to yield unimagined outcomes and affects.

In addition, contour crafting points to the possibility that buildings one day will be poured, complete with systems and structure, by one machine. Everything, from the foundation to stairs to ducts to the roof, would be integrated. The numerous systems required to put a building together—the disparate structural, cladding, finish, waterproofing, roofing, glazing, and innumerable other categories gathered in standard specification catalogs—might begin to be consolidated in favor of a few materials that are simply, intelligently varied and capable of fulfilling a multiplicity of functions. Materials and manufacturing techniques would be designed to accomplish more, reducing the number of systems required and potentially lowering the cost of building. Using techniques developed from contour crafting technology, a single house or series of different buildings could potentially be constructed in a single run, each with distinct material qualities and attributes.[02] This could allow architects, in effect, to mass customize their formations. Currently, mass customization relies on collage techniques in which the type and number of possible outcomes are controlled. The result is simply a wider variety of options from which to select—an innovation that is as substantial as personal monogramming. However, production techniques that generate more variability and respond to feedback in real time could allow the creation of non-prescribed possibilities. The next generation of manufacturing techniques based on technologies such as contour crafting will hopefully close the gap between design and actualization and will be open to greater experimentation and specification by architects.

FLEXIBLE MOLD SYSTEMS AND VARIABLE FORM-MAKING

Another technology that draws on robotics is flexible mold systems, which have been developed for the manufacture of three-dimensional laminate (3DL) sails in racing boats. A computer software package is used to design the curvature of the sail to meet precisely the wind conditions anticipated at sea. A program called Wonderware in Touch then directs a robotic machine composed of 200 actuators to shape a three-dimensional flexible mold to the calculated curvature.[03] A mylar film is laid onto the mold and a machine applies reinforcing yarns in a pattern that corresponds precisely to the computed wind load paths. Once all the yarns are laid on the base film, a second layer of film is added. The layers are then laminated using a vacuum bag and cured with a radiant heating device. Because the yarns are applied and laminated over a three-dimensional mold, they follow the same shape the sail will assume at sea.

The flexible mold technology used to create 3DL sails may have significant implications for architectural design and fabrication. By directly linking the design software to the program that controls the shape of the mold, architects can develop techniques to dynamically alter the mold as the formation is being designed. Working iteratively, designers can experiment with the feedback between the design and the limitations of the mold system. For example, an architect can test the maximum curvature allowed by the mold's robotic arms and use this information to inflect the shape of the formation. Techniques for structuring the surfaces with yarns or other strengthening fibers can also be tested in real time: the structure alters simultaneously with the shape of the formation. The production method and the mold itself evolve simultaneously, yielding affects that are both aesthetic and structural. Design and fabrication are no longer separated but are integrated into one continuous process.

Flexible mold technology also has the potential to drastically change manufacturing methods in architecture. The devices used to fabricate the sails can easily be expanded to employ heavier composite materials such as plastics and fiberglass. Curvilinear surfaces as large as an entire building envelope or as small as a single seating surface can be calculated and structured to hold their own weight and to efficiently support live and lateral wind loads. The cost of constructing curvilinear surfaces may be reduced, since each individual piece does not require its own negative mold that is only used once. Rather, a computer can be coded to adapt a single mold to a range of shapes and curvatures. By making it possible to build unique curvilinear components quickly and efficiently, flexible mold technology may go a long way towards facilitating more meaningful mass customization and the production of formations with more specific affects.

SMART MATERIALS AND MATERIAL AFFECTS

The last two technologies I want to highlight are taken from material sciences, a multidisciplinary field that explores the structural, electronic, thermal, chemical, magnetic, and optical properties of materials and their possible recombination into new composite substances. Of particular interest to technological practices are material scientists who use emergent processes similar to dynamical systems to design and

evaluate new materials. These scientists have shifted the view of materials from static substances to ones whose properties and behaviors can evolve over time. Such materials incorporate feedback into their formation, introducing an element of the virtual and opening the possibility of new outcomes and affects.

In recent years, material scientists working on developing responsive materials have begun to create a new category of substances called "smart materials."[04] These are materials that change one or more properties in response to external stimuli such as stress, heat, moisture, acidity, or alkalinity, and electric or magnetic fields. Examples include thermoresponsive materials such as shape memory alloys or polymers, which deform in response to changes in temperature and then remember their geometry within a certain temperature range. Other smart materials alter their color in response to shifts in environmental alkalinity or acidity, or to electrical, optical, or thermal stimuli. Electrochromic materials, for instance, change their color or opacity when an electrical charge is applied, while photochromic materials change color in response to light, and lighten or darken according to the amount of light. Photochromic materials are used in light sensitive spectacles that darken when exposed to bright sunlight.

The potential architectural applications of these materials are numerous. Smart materials might allow architects to develop new techniques for generating buildings that respond instantaneously to feedback from their users and environments. Directly inputting the behaviors and properties of smart materials into digital design models, for example, might enable architects to iteratively test the behavior and affects of such substances in a generative design, under various conditions of context and use. As architects research techniques to summons, control, and develop desired material properties through use, affordances between the user and formation will become interactive.

Smart materials may also have important implications for architectural fabrication techniques. Such materials already have been incorporated into devices that predict structural failure or degeneration. Some of these materials alert users to imminent collapse due to abnormal loading, corrosion, or other factors, by generating a small electrical charge that activates an alarm.

Others, such as a paint developed in Japan for use in clean rooms and other environmentally sensitive spaces, alter their porosity and chemical absorption to control pollution.[05] With further research, architects may develop new materials that can autonomously monitor and respond to environmental conditions—for example, substances that change their texture or adhesive properties to become more or less hospitable in response to either an external control or a self-regulating mechanism. As new materials capable of performing multiple functions are invented, architects may be able to do more with fewer materials. Building envelopes that currently consist of multiple layers—structure, fire resistance, soundproofing, and water membrane—could be constructed out of just one material. This could have important implications for cost as well as design and construction practices.

NANOTECHNOLOGY AND GROWING BUILDINGS

A related development of material science that holds great potential for instigating more responsive forms of architecture is nanotechnology, defined as the study of substances at the molecular or near-molecular level. Nanotechnologists explore the potential for materials to alter their fundamental behaviors and to grow and change over time.[06] For example, nanotechnologists are interested in how a heat-sensitive material may be altered at its molecular level to also respond to light, and then be induced to reproduce this behavior through self-replication. To achieve rapid self-replication, nanotechnology relies on the use of universal assemblers, molecular-scale devices that are programmed to reproduce molecular raw material at an exponential rate. In a relatively short amount of time, massive numbers of assemblers and amounts of material can be generated, allowing a transformed material characteristic to spread rapidly. In nanotechnology, several different assemblers work in concert, converging into different groups and sub-groups to produce substances organized into larger systems and more complex materials. Nano-scale growth is a bottom-up process and has an emergent aspect. The role of individual assemblers may be specified, but the product of their collective activities emerges through the process. The convergent assembly process is guided by feedback. A transmission device helps the various assemblers to communicate. Researchers have suggested that such transmission mechanisms might take the form of a polymer molecule bonded to an assembler. The polymer would function as a molecular switch with an open and closed state. Different pressures from the environment could force the switch on and off, similar to the binary operations behind computers. These transmission polymers might even be programmed to respond directly to microprocessor inputs, potentially allowing nano-scale assembly to be linked directly with digital design environments.

Techniques based on nanotechnology have the potential to alter several aspects of architecture, from transforming digital design and fabrication methods to changing the way users inhabit formations. By directly linking digital dynamical models to nanotechnology manufacturing, architects can avoid moving linearly from design techniques to actualization, and, instead, participate in a new kind of feedback loop between design and production. Architects can potentially grow buildings, scripting their molecular structure through universal assemblers. Design may become more like computer programming: occurring through the writing of scenarios and limits in anticipation of various environmental factors. This does not eliminate the role of the designer, for the architect continues to determine the goals and to analyze the results of his or her experiments. Nevertheless, the design process shifts, as the coding of formations constructed through nanotechnology will rely on iterative test runs, which inevitably yield unexpected results, forms, spaces, and affects. New techniques will be required to analyze and modify these new "grown" formations.

Nanotechnology also has the potential to alter the relationships between architectural formations and their users and contexts after a formation is actualized. Developments in smart materials already demonstrate the potential for a building's surfaces to respond in real time to environmental feedback. Nanotechnology takes these capacities even further, allowing materials to perform both sensing and actuating operations, by adopting different behaviors at various times and changing substantively their form, dimension, and organization. This adds an entirely new dimension to the practice of architecture. Virtualities become dynamic. Building envelopes can be made of materials that not only perform multiple functions, as suggested earlier, but that actually change and grow in response to environmental conditions—becoming waterproof in the event of a downpour or stronger if confronted with a sudden impact. Increased use might cause a formation's molecules to grow faster, accelerating its mutation. Surfaces may respond to users in ways both expected and unanticipated, eliciting feedback and inventive responses from users, which might cause further changes in the formation. The ability to change dynamically allows architectural formations to become catalytic to a degree previously unimaginable.

Emerging technological developments such as those discussed above offer great promise for architecture. These technologies open the imagination to tremendous possibilities: for instance, one day growing interactive buildings that change their form continually in response to feedback from their users and environments. Technologies such as virtual crash testing, contour crafting, flexible molds, smart materials, and nanotechnology all have the potential to give rise to design techniques that incorporate feedback in significant ways and to integrate design and fabrication into a single seamless process. The techniques exemplify the potentials of hybridizing technological developments from other fields with architecture. Such developments may cause tremendous catalytic effects within culture and society.

The challenge for technological practices, however, is not to wait for the arrival of radically new technologies but to develop innovative techniques with currently available machines and materials. Forecasting the future and borrowing technologies from other fields are not the ends themselves, or even direct means to an end. Instead, as I have stressed throughout this book, innovation occurs through bottom-up processes and the development of new techniques. Instead of merely looking to new technologies for analogs or examples of innovation, architects must glean operational strategies to develop techniques that incorporate feedback, destabilize their current contexts, and are process driven and interdisciplinary. These techniques enable designers to participate in a feedback loop between new technologies and developments in design. By generating new techniques, technological practices achieve a degree of flexibility that is vital to ensuring their economic survival and continued relevance in the current environment of accelerated cultural change. Techniques enable architects to move beyond merely responding to shifting milieus and allow them to actively establish new directions for technology and culture.

PROJECT 07 CATALYTIC FURNISHINGS

Multi-use Chaise
New York City, US, 2003

The chaise longue was created for an exhibition at Artists Space
Gallery in New York City. The initial aim was to create a single
piece of furniture that could support a wide range of uses in
different contexts. Thus, the formation should be adaptable
both to the environment of the gallery—where users would not be
able to sit on it—and to other contexts, such as a swimming pool
or library. We also explored ways to use a new technology, the
variable mold, to mass customize the chaise, with an eye toward
tailoring its affects to the user. A larger goal emerged: to develop
new techniques that might feed forward and affect the production
of furniture and architecture in the future.

We began by researching the relationships between surfaces and
body positions—for example, vertical planes that inspire users to
lean against them and horizontal surfaces that support lying—and
between body positions and activities. We found that body
positions allow for a range of occupations: for example, sitting,
leaning, and lying are all acceptable positions for reading, eating,
working, lounging, or sleeping, depending on the culture and
context. In some cultures, lounging may be considered permissible
at the beach but not at a dining table; in others the reverse might
be true. As our research progressed, it became evident that
relationships existed between activities, surfaces, forms, and
context, but that these connections were complex, because
individuals chose how to interact with and use each surface
depending on the situation. Our intention was to catalyze these
possibilities by creating an object that would afford the maximum
number of potential uses in the widest range of contexts.

The design of the chaise longue was initially developed through
a series of digital transformational techniques. We created a
computer model of interconnected springs that corresponded to
specific use potentials. For example, a spring connected to a
potential for leaning was attached to springs for reading and
sleeping. By adjusting the relationships between these springs
and their corresponding potentials, we developed a system in
which moving one point would produce unspecified effects to
the object's overall form. We sought to create conditions in the
formation that would encourage the body to assume unfamiliar

positions and to invent uses, thereby instigating cascading effects on other users and potentially leading to new social arrangements.

In building the chaise longue, we worked with a composite material manufacturer in China to develop FlexiMold™, a computer-controlled fabrication system capable of producing the desired surface inflections. The design of the chaise was developed simultaneously with the fabrication method. In FlexiMold, a computer directs a mold composed of 500 robotic arms to form a precise shape. The length of the pistons sets a limit on the possible formal variations. Fiberglass is laid onto the mold and redistributed to produce a monocoque shell surface of varied thickness. Numerous surface finishes are available—gel inserts can be added to the fiberglass to make it softer—creating more potential affects. FlexiMold opens several important avenues for architectural design and fabrication. First, it eliminates the need for negative molds, accelerating the manufacturing process and lowering costs. Second, it allows design and manufacturing to be integrated into a single continuous process. Designers can input variables based on a user's desires or lifestyle into a software that alters the mold in real time. Feedback occurs instantaneously: as the design changes in accordance with the architect's or client's desires, so does the mold. Each furniture piece can be customized to a user's particular lifestyle, maximizing affects for an individual rather than for a universal user. FlexiMold can also be applied to manufacture parts of buildings, allowing for the construction of complex affective forms at relatively low cost.

After the chaise is actualized[07] in metric space, the precise affordances activated depend on the user and context. An adult may sit or lounge on the formation, while a child may only be able to lean against it. Placed in the context of a library, the chaise may be used for sitting and reading. If sited next to a swimming pool, users may lie on it to sunbathe or lean against it to converse with friends. Its potentials are activated through use and invention. The techniques developed to fabricate the chaise also generate a range of affects. Methods based on the FlexiMold allow the architect to customize a formation quickly and easily to his or her design directives or to the desires of the client. FlexiMold provides an economic means to produce varied surfaces that generate undetermined affects between architecture, its users, and contexts. The technology and concomitant techniques may feed forward to influence practices in industrial design and architecture.

Performance Matrix

Range of Performance Variations

Flexible Mold Variations

A   Variation Node

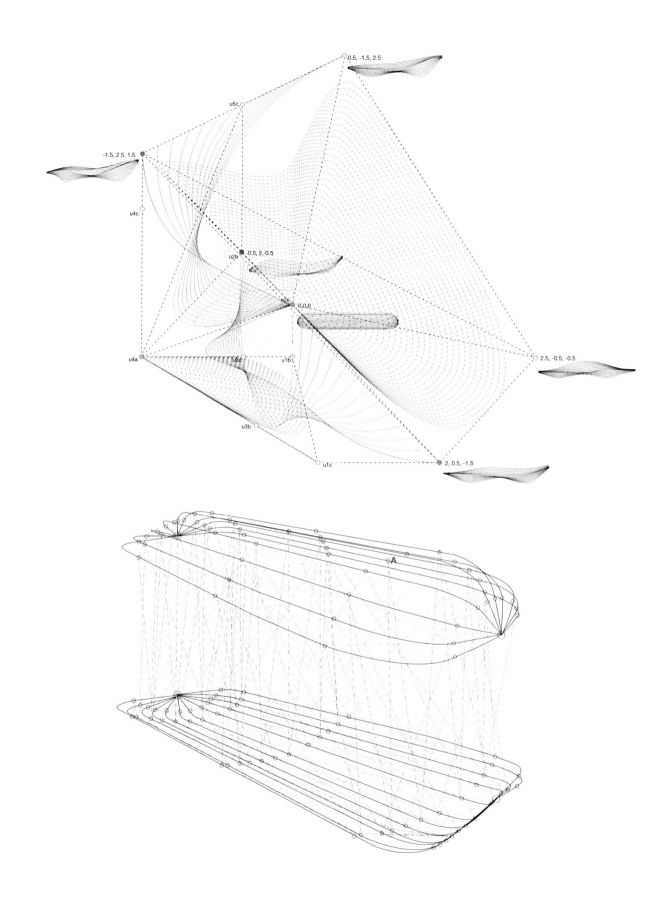

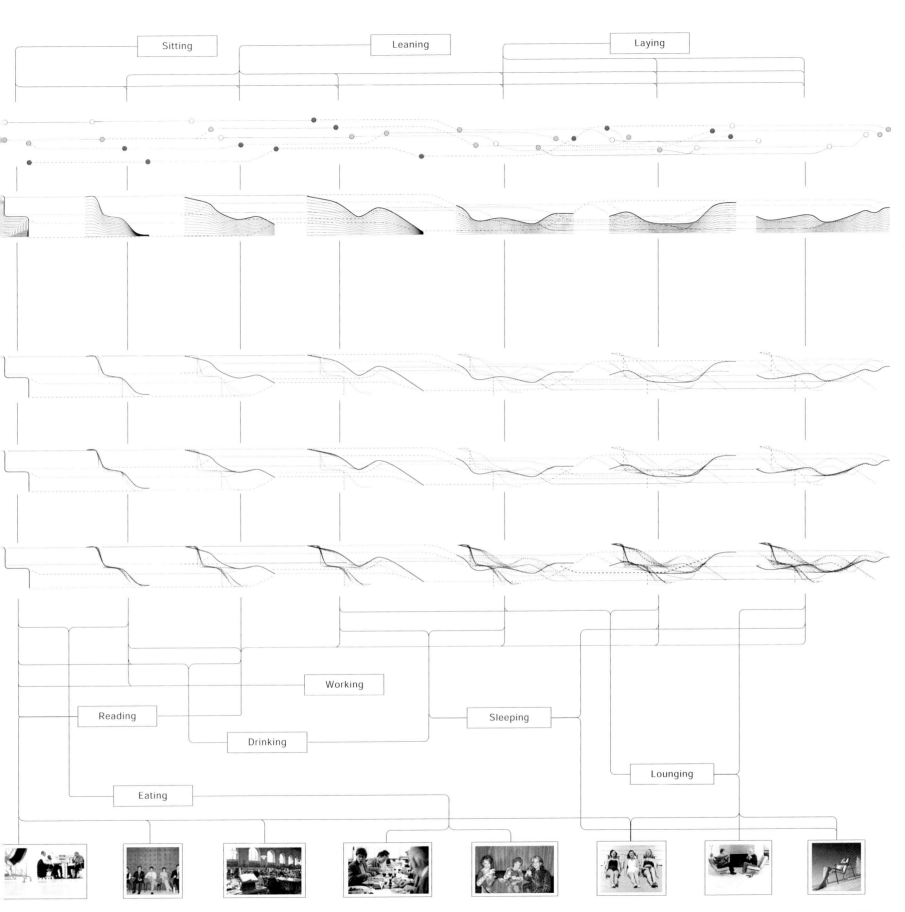

Sitting

Leaning

Laying

Working

Reading

Drinking

Sleeping

Eating

Lounging

Elevation Formation. Variation Extreme 1

Plan Formation. Variation Extreme 1

Variable Mold. Variation Extremes 1–5

A   Top of Chaise Lounge. 32 inches
B   Top of Sitting/Laying. 18 inches
C   Leaning
D   Sitting/Laying
E   Laying/Leaning
F   Leaning/Sitting

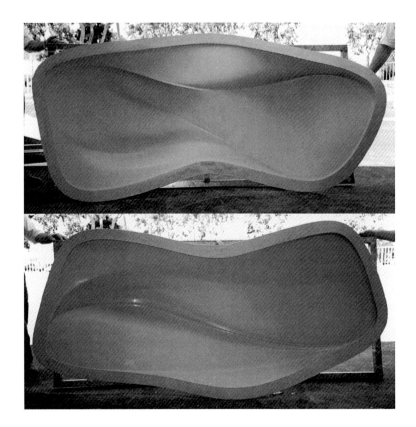

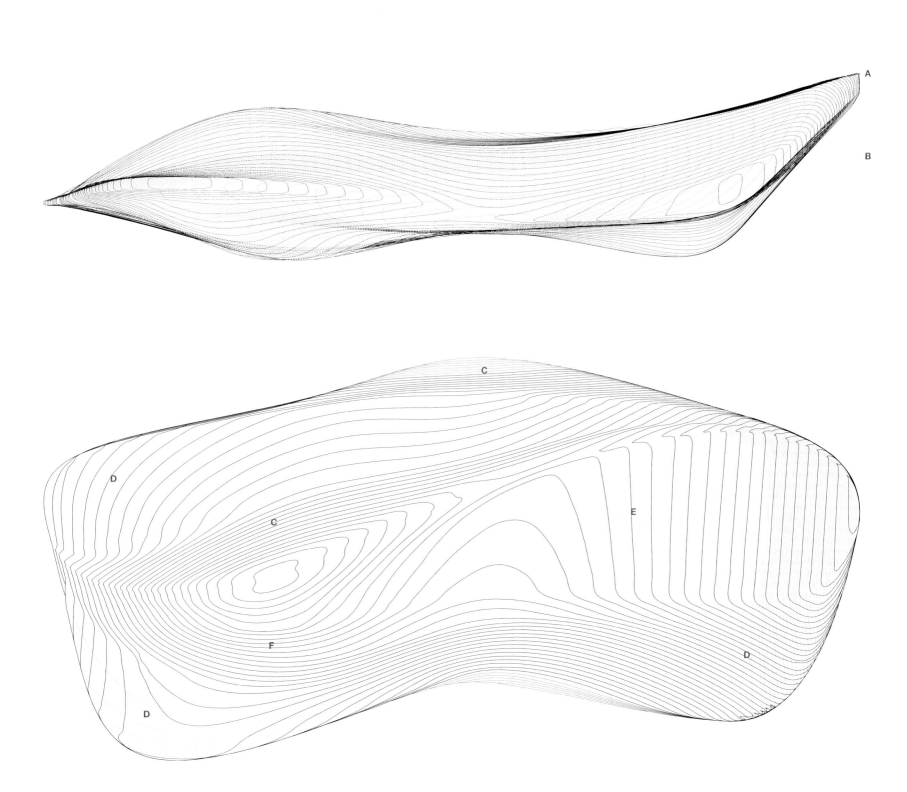

Model

Model

Model

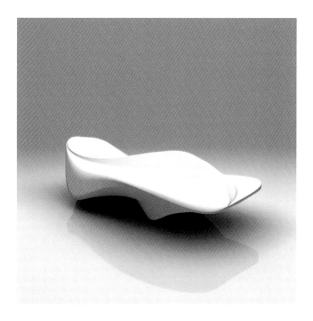

Actualized Formation in Artists Space Gallery, New York City, US, 2003

Actualized Formation in Artists Space Gallery, New York City, US, 2003

01   Virtual crash testing is one example of the development of increasingly sophisticated real-time simulations and digital software environments. Similar applications created in the digital gaming industry allow architects to consolidate material and formal parameters with performance criteria, effects, and participants. These gaming development programs facilitate real-time feedback between forms and users, permitting numerous iterations of a proposal to be evaluated and tested quickly. Kas Oosterhuis of ONL Architects has been actively using gaming software to dynamically condition architectural environments.

02   Behrokh Khoshnevis, "Automated Construction by Contour Crafting-Related Robotics and Information Technologies," in *Journal of Automation in Construction* 13, no. 1 (January 2004), 5–19.

03   *Alinghi: The Inside Story: America's Cup 2003*, Bennett Media Corporation, March 2005. [Video]

04   G. R. Tomlinson and W. A. Bullough, eds, *Smart Materials and Structures* (London: Institute of Physics Publishing, 1998).

05   Takenaka Corporation, "Paint Developed that Controls the Emission of Chemical Materials for Semiconductor and LCD Plants." Press Release, May 14, 2002. (Online: http://www.takenaka.co.jp/takenaka_e/news_e/pr0205/m0205_02.htm)

06   Eric Drexler, *Engines of Creation: The Coming Era of Nanotechnology* (Norwell, Mass.: Anchor Press, 1987).

07   For discussion of actualization, refer to page 077.

ACKNOWLEDGMENTS

This book was made possible by two grants from the University of Pennsylvania. The University of Pennsylvania Research Grant and the School of Design Grant sponsored by the Dean's office. For this I would like to thank Dean Gary Hack for his ongoing support. In addition, I would like to thank Richard Wesley for his inspiration and support during and after his time as Chair of the Architecture Department. Detlef Mertins, the current Chair of the Department of Architecture, has also been extremely supportive in encouraging the writing, designing, and publication of this book.

In addition, I have benefited from discussions with colleagues and friends over many years, including Greg Lynn, Manuel Delanda, Bill MacDonald, Enrique Norten, Patrik Schumacher, Marion Weiss, William Braham, and Winka Dubbeldam. They have stimulated and energized my teaching as well as design ideas. Special thanks go to Zaha Hadid for her support. Additionally, I would like to thank students in the design studios and seminars that I have taught over the past ten years at the University of Pennsylvania and the University of Michigan.

The team at Contemporary Architecture Practice continues to be central in providing a terrain conducive to both design research and practice. Hina Jamelle has been pivotal in helping to realize the work and ideas in this publication. Without her support this book would not have been possible.

I would also like to thank the Taylor & Francis team, especially Caroline Mallinder, Neil Warnock-Smith, and Andrew Watts with whom it has been a pleasure to work.

CR PROJECTS

Performative Leisures	Ali Rahim	Director
Leisure Center for the 2004 Olympic Games		Contemporary Architecture Practice
Athens, Greece		
Chapter 02	Julian Palacio	Design Team
	Sinan Parker	Design Team
	Yu-Chuan Chang	Design Team
	Kevin Sperry	Design Team
	Jeroen van Ameijde	Assistant
	Christopher Hoxie	Renderings
	3_D Systems	Acrylic Photopolymer Model
Inhabiting the Vector	Ali Rahim, Hina Jamelle	Directors
Reebok Flagship Store		Contemporary Architecture Practice
Shanghai, China		
Chapter 02	Jeroen van Ameijde	Design Team
	De-jan Lu	Assistant
	Kevin Sperry	Assistant
	Christopher Hoxie	Renderings
	3_D Systems	Acrylic Photopolymer Model
Variations	Ali Rahim	Director
Residence for a Fashion Designer		Contemporary Architecture Practice
London, UK		
Chapter 03	Nathaniel Hadley	Design Team
	Yu-Chuan Chang	Design Team
	Hale Everets	Design Team
	Ben Stough	Assistant
	Beatrice Witzgall	Assistant
	Jeroen van Ameijde	Assistant
	De-jan Lu	Assistant
	Christopher Hoxie	Renderings
	3_D Systems	Acrylic Photopolymer Model
Variable Porosities	Ali Rahim	Director
Digital Library		Contemporary Architecture Practice
Karachi, Pakistan		
Chapter 03	Jeroen van Ameijde	Design Team
	Kevin Sperry	Design Team
	Christopher Hoxie	Renderings
	3_D Systems	Acrylic Photopolymer Model
Migrating Coastlines	Ali Rahim, Hina Jamelle	Directors
Residential Housing Tower		Contemporary Architecture Practice
Dubai, UAE		
Chapter 04	Kevin Sperry	Design Team
	De-jan Lu	Design Team
	Pierre Alexandre de Looz	Research Assistant
	Christopher Hoxie	Renderings
	3_D Systems	Acrylic Photopolymer Model

Inflecting Potential	Ali Rahim, Hina Jamelle	Directors
Commercial Office Tower		Contemporary Architecture Practice
Dubai, UAE		
Chapter 04	Kevin Sperry	Design Team
	Christopher Hoxie	Renderings
	3_D Systems	Acrylic Photopolymer Model
Catalytic Furnishings	Ali Rahim	Director
Multi-use Chaise		Contemporary Architecture Practice
New York City, US		
Chapter 05	Julian Palacio	Design Team
	De-jan Lu	Assistant
	Hale Everets	Assistant
	Kevin Sperry	Assistant
	3_D Systems	Acrylic Photopolymer Model

CR GENERAL	Book	Dean Di Simone	Graphic Design Director
		Dean Di Simone	Cover Design
		Irene Cheng	Research Assistant
		Michael Chen	Research Assistant
		Florence Production	Graphic Production and Typesetting

Zaha Hadid Architects
Ice Storm, Vienna, Austria
Design Team:

Zaha Hadid with Patrick Schumacher
Thomas Vietzke

Marsyas
Credits:

Anish Kapoor: Artist
AGU Credits:
Cecil Balmond
Tristan Simmonds

Chapter 04   Greg Lynn FORM
Predator
Design Team:

Greg Lynn with Fabian Marcaccio
Elena Manferdini
Amanda Salud-Gallivan
Jackilin Hah
David Erdman

KOL/MAC Studio
Resi-Rise Skyscraper
Design Team:

Sulan Kolatan and William MacDonald
Stefano Colombo
Jonathan Baker
Linda Malibran
Christian Bruun
Yolanda do Campo
German Rojas
Andrew Burke
Michael Huang
Phyliss Wong
Ryan Harvey
Melodie Leung
Jose Sanchez
Beat Schenk
Marilena Komidou

Zaha Hadid Architects
Guggenheim Museum, Taichung, Taiwan
Design Team:

Zaha Hadid with Patrik Schumacher
Dillon Lin
Jens Borstelmann
Thomas Vietzke
Yosuke Hayano
Adriano De Gioannis
Delim Mimita
Juan-Ignacio Aranguren
Ken Bostock
Elena Perez
Ergian Alberg
Rocio Paz
Markus Planteu

Chapter 05

ESI Group
Virtual Crash Testing Simulation

Mark Goulthorpe dECOi
IGES Hyposurface
Design Team:

Mark Goulthorpe
Oliver Dering
Arnaud Descombes
Gabriele Evangelisti with Mark Burry
Grant Dunlop

INDEX

Pages containing relevant illustrations are indicated in **bold** type.

T - #1020 - 101024 - C232 - 254/254/12 - PB - 9781138228108 - Matt Lamination